THE ART OF

DECANTING

THE ART OF

DECANTING

BRINGING WINE TO LIFE

by **Sandra Jordan**

with Lindsey Lee Johnson *Foreword by* Robert Mondavi

CHRONICLE BOOKS

SAN FRANCISCO

Library of Congress Cataloging-in-Publication Data available.

ISBN-10: 0-8118-5679-8
ISBN-13: 978-0-8118-5679-9

Manufactured in China.

Book design by Young|Wells
Photographs by Caitlin McCaffrey, unless otherwise noted.

Distributed in Canada by Raincoast Books
9050 Shaughnessy Street
Vancouver, British Columbia V6P 6E5

10 9 8 7 6 5 4 3 2 1

Chronicle Books LLC
680 Second Street
San Francisco, California 94107

www.chroniclebooks.com

End pages: The Jordan Estate, Healdsburg, California

To my husband Tom, who has dutifully listened as I have spun my 1,001 tales of the history and lore of our joint passion, wine and the history of the decorative arts.

I know we share the hope that this tome helps preserve and propagate these cherished, time-honored traditions, while bringing together friends and family.

May these ceremonies run like a golden thread through the course of your lives, weaving together the treasured moments, leaving a dazzling tapestry of joyful memories.

SJ

CONTENTS

FOREWORD *by Robert Mondavi*   9

INTRODUCTION   11

THE MAGIC THAT HAPPENS BETWEEN
THE BOTTLE AND THE GLASS: *Decanting*   15

SERVING AND STORING WINE OVER TIME: *Vessels*   37

CHILLING WINE WITH STYLE: *Wine Coolers and Monteiths*   53

PROTECTED FOR AGES, FREE IN A MOMENT: *Corks and Corkscrews*   63

AN ELEGANT DISPLAY: *Wineglasses*   77

THE GREATEST PLEASURE: *Tasting and Appreciating Wines*   89

BEYOND BASIC: *Furnishings for Fine Wines*   99

FROM THE VINEYARD TO THE TABLE: *A Vintner's Dinner*   107

EPILOGUE *by Rob Davis*   124

ACKNOWLEDGMENTS   125

BIBLIOGRAPHY   126

PHOTO AND ILLUSTRATION CREDITS   128

INDEX   130

FOREWORD

Robert Mondavi and Sandra Jordan

There's something special about life in California's wine country. It is the generous bounty that nature provides us here—the benevolent weather, the uncommon beauty of the land, and the closeness to the vineyards, the source of our lifestyle. It is the feeling one gets here, the sense of warmth, and the timeless enjoyment of all things simple and good. The wine country is a place for gatherings of friends and family, offerings of good food, the appreciation of music and art, and reverence for eras gone by. And, of course, there is the wine.

From cellaring to tasting, each step in the journey from the vine to the glass rewards us in many ways. To learn about these steps is not only to expand your knowledge of wine but also to enhance and enrich your own lifestyle. It's fascinating to discover how these rituals began, to understand the ways in which each generation has contributed to making the experience of drinking and sharing wine ever more delightful.

The Art of Decanting: Bringing Wine to Life has been researched and produced by the Jordan Vineyard & Winery in celebration of the great wine traditions: the rituals, techniques, and accoutrements of wine service that have been part of sophisticated societies since the time of the ancients. Many of these traditions provide practical benefits to the wine as well as ceremony for those seated at the table, making for an enjoyable wine experience that is fondly recalled for years afterward.

Is there anything in life that is better than truly fond memories? As hosts, we hope to create such memories, both for ourselves and for our guests. We delight in experiencing wonderful evenings among friends, filled with talk and laughter. I hope that you will bring the age-old ceremonies of decanting and serving to your table—and share the first taste of an exceptional wine with the people you care for most. This is the good life.

On its fifteen-hundred-acre Alexander Valley estate, Jordan Vineyard & Winery has been consistently crafting elegant, approachable Cabernet Sauvignon and Chardonnay for more than twenty-five years. Like the Jordan family, I believe that the traditions of the wine country should be treasured and preserved. After all, they are part of our rich cultural heritage—our link to the past, and our cherished gift for the future.

Robert Mondavi
Founder, Robert Mondavi Winery

INTRODUCTION

There is a certain ineffable tinge of joy and anticipation that we feel in our hearts when we hear the unmistakable "pop" of a wine bottle as it is opened. That magical sound uncorks a wave of delicious sensations and memories and heralds new ones to come. For wine is a treasure to be enjoyed in good company. Each bottle is a celebration—of the bounty of the harvest, the fruit of one's labors, of life itself.

When you hear that marvelous little noise, the cares of the day gently ebb away. The twilight is suffused not only with the glorious colors of sunset but also with the tantalizing scents of dinner and the merry din of conversation. Each time I hear that sound, I want to dive into the moment and draw it out, savoring each delightful sense.

And so it was with great pleasure that I discovered the art of decanting. Equal parts romance and ceremony, decanting is a time-honored tradition. From the Egyptians, who embellished their clay *amphorae* with elaborate descriptions of a wine's origins and qualities, to the Victorians, who sipped their wine from lavish glassware, wine lovers have long cherished the rituals surrounding the storage and service of wine. Today, in our homes, we continue to honor these esteemed traditions.

The great beauty of decanting, though, lies in its simplicity. One requires neither expensive tools nor elaborate training to properly present and serve wine. In basic terms, decanting is the pouring of wine into a glass container to aerate the wine and reduce sediment. However, the charms of this art are not limited to the palate. The exquisite display of cascading wine is thrilling to watch and heightens the anticipation of that first sip.

In the pages that follow, I have sought to delve into and share the pleasures of presenting, serving, and sharing wine. Traveling through history to understand the rituals and the many opinions regarding their role and enjoyment, *The Art of Decanting: Bringing Wine to Life* is a journey of discovery. We explore the spirited debates that have long been swirling around the art of serving and enjoying a fine wine, listening to the voices of world-renowned connoisseurs such as Hugh Johnson, Emile Peynaud, Gerald Asher, Robert Mondavi, Ray Duncan, and my husband, Tom Jordan.

Whether you are a novice taster or a discriminating oenophile, *The Art of Decanting: Bringing Wine to Life* offers an illuminating portrait of the ceremonies and accoutrements that enhance the sensory pleasures of wine. Among the intriguing questions we entertain are the following:

Should one decant only an older wine? What about a young one?

Can improperly decanting a vintage library wine lead to its ruin? Or are such aged wines far less flavorful if they are not decanted?

Should one quickly transfer wine from the decanter to the glass? Or wait
as long as several hours for the right moment to imbibe?

Can the shape of a glass enhance the taste of a wine? Will the wrong glass taint it?

Above all, we seek to understand how to maximize the enjoyment of each sip of wine.

The next time you open a bottle of wine, take a moment to look around at the faces of
your friends and family members—each will be suffused with a radiant glow of excitement,
anticipation, and joy. And that is truly worth savoring.

Cheers,

Sandra Jordan
Creative Director, Jordan Vineyard & Winery

THE MAGIC THAT HAPPENS BETWEEN
THE BOTTLE AND THE GLASS

DECANTING

W HEN AND WHERE DID DECANTING BEGIN?

When did humankind add this essential step in the rituals of serving and enjoying wine, discovering that wine and air could be such a glorious combination?

Perhaps the best place to start our search is with the *amphora*. Invented by the Canaanites sometime before 1500 B.C., this basic clay container became ubiquitous in the ancient world. Egyptians, Greeks, and Romans alike stored wine in amphorae, and with this invention they could, for the first time, tote a manageable quantity of wine to the table, break the clay seal, and pour a drink for an eager guest.

However, if a guest had been so eager as to drink straight from this ancient vessel, he would have found himself with a mouthful of misery. In a time when winemaking was still a primitive process, and aging a dodgy proposition, raw wine would have been extraordinarily thick, not to mention encumbered by a great deal of sediment.

Ancient Egyptians sieved their wine in order to ameliorate these problems, and at gatherings they employed lovely young girls to pour and serve from the decorative vessels (perhaps to distract guests' attention from the taste of the wine). The *amphora* may have made wine portable, but it did not make it potable.

Not surprisingly, it was the ever-ingenious Greeks who, when not busy inventing philosophy and democracy, developed the idea of wine blending. Here we see decanting taken to the extreme: Wine was poured into *kraters* (mixing bowls used

The amphora was an all-purpose vessel used by the ancient Egyptians, Greeks, and Romans, but it is best remembered for carrying wine.

An Egyptian banquet scene depicts the use of amphorae in the ancient world.

omment le noble roy alixandre fu empoisonne
laquelle poison il termina ce par mort. xlij

ous auez bien oy par cy deuant comment
alixandre auoit enuoye par tous les reg
monde ses lettres as seigneurs pour estre a

exclusively for this purpose), where it was not only aerated but also blended with sea water, spices, and aromatics. They used this method at the legendary *symposium,* a Greek drinking party at which men gathered to lounge upon lavish sofas, debate, carouse, and enjoy each other's company—along with a hearty quantity of blended wine. "Wine was always mixed with water. To drink it undiluted was the mark of a barbarian," writes wine historian Nina Wemyss. One can only imagine what today's sommelier would have to say about such an exercise if a valuable vintage were involved. Nevertheless, these ancient hosts had set the standard: Wines, not yet sophisticated enough to stand alone, would be carefully prepared before they were proudly served.

The tradition of blending wine reemerged in the rustic dining halls of medieval England, where wines were also decanted and combined with water. Medieval wine servers added a third step to the process, flavoring wines at the *aumbry,* an early sideboard. One account enumerating the many medieval servers mentions a ewerer (to pour water), a butler (to oversee wine decanting and spicing), and a cup bearer (to bring the treated wine to the table). The fact that it was deemed right and proper to add anything to a wine for drinking may tell us something about the tenacity of social tradition and ritual (the idea having started so long before, with the Greeks); it also tells us something about the wine's palatability—or lack thereof.

As the centuries passed and the quality of wine improved, the high-drama rituals of blending wine with water would eventually give way to a new, more refined table show: blending wine with air.

On a Greek vessel, a slave holds a ladle and an elegant wine cup called a kylix.

A Greek krater, used for mixing wine and water, features images of music, women, and wine.

In medieval England, decanting wine became a highly specialized ritual.

In the restful confines of the bottle, the wine awaits maturity as youth gives way to wisdom.

—PEGGY FURTH,
Vice Chairman,
Chalk Hill Estates
Vineyards & Winery,
Healdsburg, California

The flavors have been locked in for so long. Sometimes, the wine needs to open up.

—JUSTIN HALL,
Sommelier,
Charlie Trotter's, Chicago

By the seventeenth and eighteenth centuries, wood barrels and glass bottles had become the universal vessels for wine. However, the wine they contained was still, as Hugh Johnson writes, "expected to be a bit murky." One such example was the mid-seventeenth-century British favorite, port. The thick texture and sometimes heavy sediment of this sweet beverage (which was at that time the wine most readily available and not yet considered strictly a dessert wine) made it a prime candidate for decanting, and thus the tradition was revived.

The late eighteenth and early nineteenth centuries saw the arrival of the golden age of decanting, with Madeira its primary cause and beneficiary. Produced on the island of Madeira, this particular wine made its way to America's shores during the Colonial era, and there it stayed. The reason? Cromwell's Navigation Act of 1651, in which the British government declared that the American colonies should trade with no one but England herself, meant that American ships had to make regular trips across the Atlantic. For reasons no longer known, King Charles allowed one exception to this rule, permitting American trade with the island of Madeira, conveniently located along the Atlantic sea route. During the following decades, trade ships en route to and from the colonies frequently stopped over in Madeira and loaded their ships with wine. Hence, the wine that had been made in Madeira and survived the long sea voyage to England or America found a regular and esteemed place on the tables of both nations.

Madeira soon asserted its affinity for decanting, for two main reasons. First, the hold of a creaky Colonial trade ship would have been damp, dank, and turbulent. Not the ideal setting for a settling wine, surely, but the Atlantic journey was long, and if one factor leads to the accumulation of sediment, it is time. By the time a bottle of Madeira reached the dining room of an American host, it was in need of some care and consideration—to be released from its dirty, dusty bottle at the very least. Second, the uncommon beauty and color of Madeira (a deep, golden amber) is visually striking and calls out to be prominently displayed.

Once decanting was firmly rooted in the American and British table traditions, savvy wine merchants helped to foster and develop what had, in essence, begun with the ancients: *a culture of wine*. Decanting was essential to this world of wine; among the desirable new *objets* were crystal decanters from English glass houses, as well as "bottle tickets"—small silver tags that hung from the necks of decanters and demurely announced their contents.

Decanters appear frequently in literary and historical accounts of the eighteenth and nineteenth centuries. These range from a British professor's diary of undergraduate ribaldry at St. Stephen's ("When the decanter came round to anyone, if it was nearly emptied, the next in succession could require him to finish it . . . ") to Ebenezer Scrooge's fictional experience with the drink ("Headmaster produced a decanter of curiously light wine . . .") to the Black Bottle affair of 1840 (in which James Brudenell, Seventh Earl of Cardigan, was enraged to find, on the table at a formal mess dinner, a bottle of wine rather than a decanter—a faux pas that resulted in the arrest of the offending party, one Captain Reynolds). Clearly, by the height of the Victorian era, decanting was not just the fashionable way—but also the only way—to serve wine.

Riedel decanter with stopper and bottle ticket.

Bottle tickets were widely used in the mid-nineteenth century.

Why Decant? The Risks and Rewards of a Ritual

Like a prized rose, a fine wine sometimes needs a little finesse to blossom. A young red may resemble a tight bud, its full flavor and aroma waiting to be released. An older vintage may have bloomed to its fullest splendor but carry with it unwanted sediment. In rare cases, young whites may contain an excess of free sulfur dioxide and thus give off a slight odor. And certainly both mature whites and reds may suffer from a lack of oxygen. The ritual of decanting can address all of these problems.

The basic effect of decanting is a great release. The wine, which has matured under the cloak of cellar and bottle glass, now meets fresh air. Though debates continue over whether decanting is helpful, harmful, or ineffectual, it can be generally stated that decanting will mellow a young red and draw out the flavors in a mature red, and that white wines do not usually require decanting.

Even with these simple truths established, the controversy carries on. Vintage library wines, in particular, are treasured by oenophiles, and thus the idea of decanting them provokes strong opinions on all sides. Some experts recommend decanting for older wines that have yielded a good deal of sediment. Justin Hall, sommelier at Charlie Trotter's, points out that an older wine may also need to be drawn out, through decanting, as much as a younger one. "The flavors have been locked in for so long," he says. "Sometimes, the wine needs to open up."

In his book *Vineyard Tales: Reflections on Wine*, wine expert Gerald Asher relates the story of just such a successful release through decanting: "Not too long ago I served a Beringer Napa Valley

Appreciating old wine is like making love to a very old lady. It is possible. It can even be enjoyable. But it requires a bit of imagination.

—ANDRE TCHELISTCHEFF, Winemaker, talking to Michael Broadbent on tasting a 1797 Lafite

A long-cellared bottle awaits its moment in the decanter.

Private Reserve Cabernet Sauvignon '86 at a dinner party," he writes. "The wine was tough and decidedly tannic when I first drew the cork, but two hours in a decanter tamed the tannin and brought out a rich aroma and flavor we might not otherwise have enjoyed. The wine was gorgeous when it could have been what is politely called a challenge." Asher believes that red wine needs to be aerated to be enjoyed at its best. "I now decant red wines as a matter of course," he writes.

Those who value fleshier, more powerful wines worry that decanting these old vintages and exposing them to the air for too long could steal their last breaths and leave them tasting faded. Peter Marks of Napa Valley's Copia prefers to err on the side of caution when dealing with these precious older wines. "[An older] wine can get old and tired very quickly if it is allowed to sit in the decanter for too long," he warns. "It's better to get it right in the glass to be consumed quickly."

Some say that young wines benefit most from the exposure to oxygen, which can massage the wine to soften bitter tannins and quickly draw out more intense aromas and flavors. Surely, if one wishes to explore the possibilities of decanting, it's preferable to begin with a less expensive, more readily available young red wine. More vigorous than a library wine, a young red can stand up to the air quite well—and will likely benefit from it.

In truth, the beneficial influence of air upon young reds may be the closest thing to a certainty in the world of decanting. In all other matters—particularly in those pertaining to treasured library wines—the experts continue to engage in fierce debate and friendly disagreement.

The Art of Decanting, sculpture by Gerard Puvis, 2003.

The discovery of a wine is of greater moment than the discovery of a constellation. The universe is too full of stars.

—BENJAMIN FRANKLIN

I like to decant thirty minutes to an hour ahead of time. I actually like to experience a wine as it develops, rather than afterward, which can happen when you decant too early.

—CAROLINE STYNE,
Owner and Sommelier,
AOC Wine Bar, Los Angeles

Baby Bacchus Decanting,
by Margrit Biever Mondavi, 2006

With the myriad of opinions about whether and when to decant, it can be difficult to decide how to treat a premium old vintage. The best and safest option is to decant a mature wine "on the spot," or at the table, in a sensual ritual of care and precision that heightens the anticipation accompanying a fine, well-aged red. Because these wines tend to be more volatile than young ones, mere seconds in the air will release layers of bouquet and flavor. If the wine, upon meeting the air, still needs more time to fully develop, then one may certainly allow it to settle in the decanter while another bottle is served, returning to the older vintage at a later point in the meal.

A moderately mature wine (generally, a red six to eight years old) will benefit from more time spent in the decanter—as much as an hour, though as little as fifteen seconds will do some good. For a young wine (a red one to five years old), however, consider decanting one to three hours before your dinner to allow more oxygen to reach the wine, unleash the flavors, and smooth out the texture. In short, some patience, and a good decanter, can improve the flavor and bouquet of a rough young red immeasurably.

To decant as a host is pleasurable; to experience this ritual as a guest can be an unequalled luxury, an opportunity to both observe and absorb its intricacies. Master sommeliers have such a depth of knowledge and experience that they can often properly judge, decant, and serve a fine wine using pure intuition. In a fine restaurant, the sommelier should be able to advise diners regarding whether, when, and how to decant a particular wine. In some cases, a thoughtful host may enhance the dining experience by ordering the wine for a special meal

The height of elegance, Hugh Johnson's Ship's Decanter, based on an eighteenth-century design, allows a fine wine gentle exposure to the air.

Anyone who can pour wine into a glass can decant a bottle of wine.

—GERALD ASHER,
Vineyard Tales: Reflections on Wine, 1996

In the ritual of enjoying a fine bottle of wine, to miss the step of decanting would be much like forgoing a sensual prelude to an evening of lovemaking.

—H. WILLIAM HARLAN,
Proprietor, Harlan Estates, Oakville, California

early—even as much as a day in advance—in case a significant aeration period is recommended.

But a caveat to all who cherish a fine wine: the effect of decanting is unpredictable. "Wines can be hurt or helped by decanting," Hall says. However, with most wines, the benefits of decanting seem to outweigh the risks. One must simply decant a wine with care, and then, once the wine is in the decanter, enjoy it in all of its fascinating stages: as it opens and expands, blossoms and ripens, lives and retires, with the air.

I encourage one to decant young wines, old wines, and many of those wines in between.

—CHRISTOPHER P. LAVIN,
Sommelier, L'Opera,
Long Beach, California

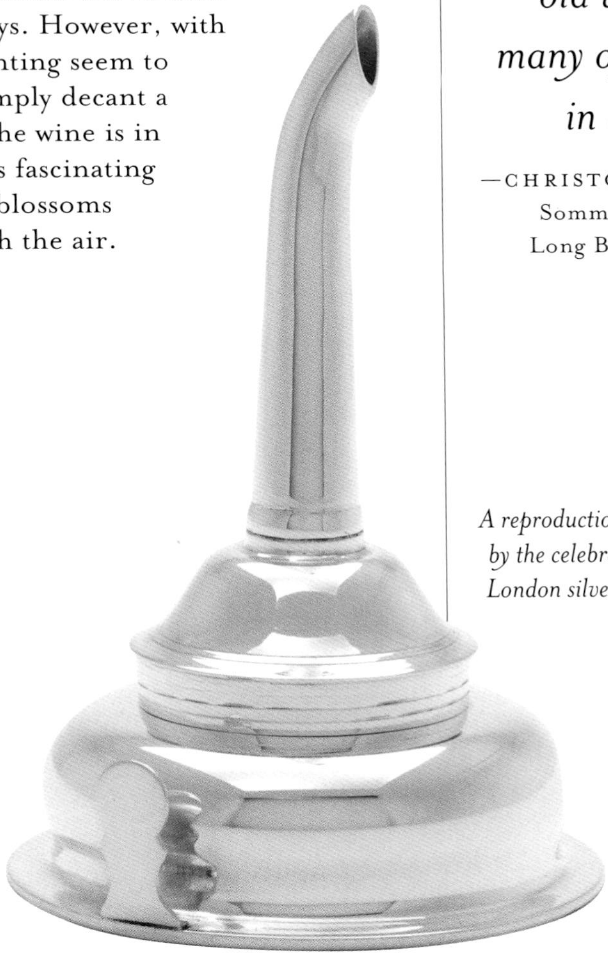

A reproduction of a wine funnel made by the celebrated eighteenth-century London silversmith Hester Bateman.

I have found that the best way to decant and serve an older bottle is to take it carefully from its cellar resting place, bring it carefully to the table, stand it up to uncork, then gently pour it over the candle into the decanter.

—MARC S. GARNER,
Wine Director, Ringside
Steakhouse, Portland, Oregon

THE BOTTLE, THE CANDLE, AND THE DECANTER: HOW TO DECANT

Though its effect on wine may be complex, decanting itself is relatively simple. First, the host or sommelier removes the bottle's capsule and cork with a gentle hand and then wipes the lip. He places a candle on the table near the decanter, where the soft light will illuminate the sediment as it moves through the liquid. (Some sommeliers use a flashlight for this purpose, and, while it works well, it can detract from the warm ambience of the decanting ritual.) Holding the bottle at an angle above the flame, he slowly pours the wine into the decanter in one continuous motion. Pouring so that the liquid runs down the inside of the decanter ensures that the wine will not splash into the decanter and tire. When the sediment reaches the lower neck of the bottle, he ceases pouring and stands the bottle upright.

When all the wine has been poured, the ritual is usually complete, though some sommeliers have been rumored to shake the decanter to more fully aerate the wine—a controversial move, to put it mildly. (Hugh Johnson declared that he should faint if he saw this.) Purists, especially when they are presenting a fine old vintage, will decant with the utmost care in order to leave the wine as undisturbed as possible. Some professionals will even rinse out the original bottle and decant the wine back into it in order to present the wine with its label and thus preserve its identity at table.

But is pouring wine into a decanter all there is to this tradition? Gracious hosts and grateful guests have known the answer for centuries: accessories such as wine coasters and funnels are indispensable tools in the elegant service of wine.

Step 1: The host presents the bottle to his guests.

Step 3: He gently uncorks the bottle.

Step 2: He removes the foil from the capsule.

Step 4: He decants the wine in a slow, continuous pour.

An antique papier-mâché coaster.

An antique pierced-silver coaster.

An Alexander Valley silver coaster.

An antique silver coaster, in the Sheffield style.

An antique papier-mâché coaster.

A Healdsburg magnum silver coaster.

An antique Georgian silver coaster.

A pierced silver coaster, in the Sheffield style.

A silver-plated coaster, in the Sheffield style.

For a special touch at a modern dinner party, a host may wish to set both decanters and bottles on beautiful wine coasters arranged on the table, with a nod to wine aficionados from centuries past. These coasters originated, like so many wine traditions, in the eighteenth century. As is still true today, servers were not always immediately at hand, even in the grandest houses, and impatient and often-raucous guests would slide the wine decanters to and fro across the table to serve themselves. From this rather inelegant practice came the very elegant wine coaster, a small, circular tray with high sides made to hold the decanter and protect the table or cloth from nicks and stains. The Victorians, being themselves, soon took this as a new opportunity for lavish decoration, and the wine coaster became a silver, gold, or lacquered papier-mâché item used mainly for display. Artisans responded by developing coaster wagons or boats, jolly little wheeled carts that could truck two decanters of wine around the table, requiring minimal effort on the part of thirsty guests.

The right wine funnel can also make a difference in the serving and drinking of a fine wine. Usually silver, the funnel rests atop the decanter and makes the decanting process slightly less precarious. A cranked spout, or curved tip, is essential, since it deflects wine down the sides of the decanter and thus exposes it to more oxygen. Wine funnels are usually equipped with strainers or filters, pierced in decorative patterns, and one can also stretch a piece of muslin or cheesecloth (avoiding filters made from paper products) across the opening to catch the finest impurities, sediment, and bits of stray cork. A glinting silver funnel, paired with an elegant glass decanter and coaster, can be a visually stunning addition to any table.

[Wine] cheers the sad, revives the old, inspires the young, makes weariness forget his toil.

—LORD BYRON, *Sardanapalus, a Tragedy,* 1821

The wine coaster was so named because the circular stands "coasted" around the table.

Perhaps the most treasured moment of a feast is this, the moment just after decanting. Before a sip is taken, before a morsel is tasted, it is wonderful to stand before a table full of friends, with the promise of a fine, entertaining meal ahead. The decanter stands upon the table; full now, its bounty expands, in scent and flavor, with the air. The color, depths of vivid red or hues of gold, shines in the clear glass. The guests are now served one by one, wine poured generously into each waiting glass, and as each takes his or her first delicate sip the host may enjoy a taste as well, cherishing this feeling, the quiet, warm pleasure of a tradition well served.

Wines are living history and bring old traditions and new friends together.

—SHELLEY LINDGREN,
Wine Director and
General Manager,
A16 restaurant, San Francisco

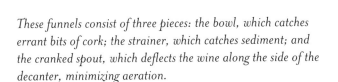

These funnels consist of three pieces: the bowl, which catches errant bits of cork; the strainer, which catches sediment; and the cranked spout, which deflects the wine along the side of the decanter, minimizing aeration.

A selection of wine funnels, an essential decanting accessory.

SERVING AND STORING WINE OVER TIME

VESSELS

THE STORY OF WINE VESSELS,

like that of decanting, begins in clay—with the amphora. Crude in material and basic in design, this wine vessel was one of the most important and frequently used objects in the ancient world. Today, amphorae are oft-discovered archaeological treasures, emerging from King Tutankhamen's tomb (thirty-six of them), lying under the long-settled dust of Pompeii, depicted in ancient stone and marble relief scenes, and, broken in shards, spread across the beaches of the Aegean Sea.

Because it allowed for the limited aging and easy transportation of wine, the amphora was a revolutionary object, which was essential to the development of decanting. It was also the first in a long line of vessels made to store and serve wine, a family of vessels that became more refined with the years, culminating in the most useful wine carrier the world has seen: the modern cylindrical glass bottle.

When one looks at the vessel that started it all, the amphora, what is most remarkable is its simplicity. Its clay is unglazed and untreated—except for an inner coating of resin that protects the wine from the fatal dangers of light, heat, and evaporation. In truth, there are two types of amphorae: the one-piece amphora, with a short neck and bloated oval body, and the neck amphora, whose elongated neck rises from a heart-shaped body. In both types, a handle is secured to each side of the neck, which widens into a belly meant for holding wine and then tapers to form a pointed foot. Some experts believe that there were likely practical reasons for this foot: It may have

Ancient Roman vessels, such as these from Margrit and Robert Mondavi's private collection, took on many different forms, including animal shapes.

These two-handled amphorae were the main vessels for wine transportation in early days.

allowed the vessels to be stacked on their sides for storage on trade ships, much like wine bottles are stored in cellars today, and it may have also acted as an extra handle that made the amphora easier to carry.

The amphora may rightly be considered a treasure of history. Without it, wine would not have had a proper place to age and, without the aging process, what we call wine would be a mere syrup made from crushed grapes. We can also say with certainty that without aging there would be no sediment—and without sediment, no primary cause for decanting, which is now such a vital part of serving wine.

The ancient Greeks' krater (see page 16) represents another important stage in the development of wine vessels. Used for mixing wine with spices and water, it also served as a grand ceremonial centerpiece. We can think of the krater as a very early ancestor of the sideboard (see page 103) or even of today's gleaming mahogany bar. It was the host's proud station, the place from which his guests were served, and it was appropriately beautiful. Kraters that have survived the centuries showcase enticing details of Greek life and myth, from depictions of frivolity and wine drinking to scenes from Homer's *Odyssey*. Whatever their decoration, these grand mixing bowls are intricately weaved with the social history of the Greeks and their wine.

Equally beautiful, though today more likely to be imagined than seen, were the jeweled and metallic wine vessels of seventeenth-century Persian royalty. In 1673, French diarist Sir John Chardin stepped into the opulent and fantastic-sounding world of the Safavid monarch Shah Abbas II, and

Both decorative and useful, the krater was the centerpiece of the Greek symposium. Depicted here are two types of kraters: the stamnos *(top) and the* pelike *(bottom).*

These elegantly crafted blue-hued Roman beakers and cups date from the second to fourth century A.D.

A Roman glass jug circa third century A.D.

A Roman flask circa third century A.D.

A Roman wine pitcher circa fourth century A.D.

the nobleman was eager to record the wonders he beheld there. If we take Chardin's accounts as truth, then the wine served by the Shah of Persia may have enjoyed more luxurious surroundings than almost any beverage in history. Chardin recalls meeting with the Shah's head "Purveyor of Wine" and produces for readers a list of dozens upon dozens of vessels and drinking cups, flagons, ladles, salvers, dishes, and more—all of gold, some jewel-encrusted, others set with pearls. He writes, "It is incredible, the vast Quantity, and the Value . . . there are Cups so large, that one cannot hold them in one Hand when they are full. . . . No part of the World," he writes, "can afford any thing [sic] more magnificent and rich, or more splendid and bright."

There may have been nothing more bright than the Shah's golden cups, but by the latter part of the seventeenth century Western Europe had produced something just as splendid—at least as far as wine itself was concerned—the glass bottle.

Prior to the invention of the glass bottle in the 1660s, the world had seen similarly shaped vessels, but in earthenware and stoneware. One of these, the bellarmine, named for the Counter-Reformationist Cardinal Roberto Bellarmino, was a muddy, mottled brown jug with a slim neck, balloon body, flat bottom, and salted glaze. Other vessels of this shape included earthenware bottles, attractive white-glazed jugs with handles and labels (with the type and year of the wine scribed in blue glaze across the jug's broad belly). Despite the charm of these early examples, they were simply no match for the transparency, utility, and uncomplicated beauty of glass.

Glass has been at least as important as clay in the long history of wine, and its rise in popularity forever altered the way we drink. With the glass bottle came an ideal place for wine to age safely, the development of standardized shapes and quantities of wine, and new opportunities to put wine on display. And with the glass bottle came another essential development in the history of wine presentation: the glass decanter.

It's impossible to say how frequently, in those early days, glass bottles were used to decant wine and glass decanters were used to contain it. What is clear, however, is that both vessels became increasingly popular during the ensuing centuries and that both changed as the times changed, each growing into the optimal shape for its particular purpose.

The "shaft and globe," a shape that was used for early bottles and decanters alike, resembles a bloated Eiffel Tower: a wide bottom tapers upward to a narrow neck. In its basic shape, one can detect traces of the neck amphora of earlier times.

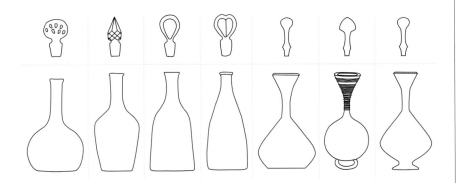

Shoulder and taper decanters, popular for centuries, are still in use today.

Strange as it may seem, there never was a word coined in France for "decanter." They have the verb décanter *for "to decant," but nothing better than* carafe *has to do for both wine and water.*

—ANDRÉ L. SIMON,
Author and wine authority

Engraving adds interest to Baccarat's Sévigné glass shoulder decanter.

This Hugh Johnson three-ring decanter is based on a design from the 1790s.

As time passed, glassmakers experimented with both decanters and bottles, and they achieved some interesting results. The decanter largely retained its shaft-and-globe shape, but this shape became more refined, with more elegant lines drawn from the neck to the body. Ornamentation made a difference as well; we see examples of engraved glass (some of these decanters display the names of wines etched into their glass, others sport grape leaves, and still others feature elaborate crests) as well as cut glass, with a more dramatic, ridged look.

There was a brief, rather strange divergence sometime in the early 1700s: the cruciform decanter, which looks like four rectangular bottles joined together under one neck. It has been speculated that this vessel was used for chilling wine, because it allowed more wine to touch glass. There were also angular shoulder decanters and tall, elegant taper decanters, both of which are still made and sold today. However, the ship's decanter (which is depicted on the cover of this book) is now the favored alternative, if not for its usefulness (the wine runs smoothly down the long neck, settling but not splashing in the wide bottom) then for its classic, clean-lined beauty.

As for the bottle, its journey was an evolution upward: from the decanter-like shaft and globe, the bottle was gradually tamped down into the "onion" shape, which was widely popular by the year 1700. Let us hope that this particular shape never makes a comeback: with a short tapered neck, fat round body, and murky brown color, the bottle is a fair candidate for its name and brings to mind Falstaff at the pub, not King Henry at court. Fortunately for all, however, the "onion" gave way to the "mallet," as glass bottles stretched and narrowed. The change was gradual but consistent; slow and steady improvements

Decanters adorn the table in Gawen Hamilton's painting The Brothers Clarke with Other Gentlemen Taking Wine, *circa 1730–35.*

resulted as the bottle moved closer and closer to what it was destined, of course, to become: the tall, elegant glass cylinder.

Why the cylinder? By the 1740s, vintners, who had discovered the invaluable cork (see page 64), had also seen the essential truth: in order to prevent the cork from drying out and shrinking up, the wine must be stored on its side. The cylindrical bottle is perfectly shaped for this purpose—much like the amphora, centuries before.

We may view the glass bottle as today's amphora, the best vessel yet invented for storing wine and bringing it to the table. The bottle, like its ancient predecessor, is present at every feast, yet it is only the first step in properly serving wine. The glass decanter is the bottle's best ally, for it receives the bottle's precious cargo and opens it to the edifying air. Together, the glass bottle and decanter have become what the amphora once was: wine's most valuable aid. With care and time and luck, they regularly create miracles, transforming an acceptable amalgamation of grapes into something extraordinary.

Early glass wine bottles could not be easily stored on their sides, due to their "onion" and "mallet" shapes.

The evolution of the wine bottle: modern bottles (facing page) and antique bottles dating from circa 1640 to 1850 (above).

> *For several months after bottling, fine wines are often in a sort of state of dumb shock. They seem to sulk.*
>
> —HUGH JOHNSON,
> *How to Enjoy Wine*, 1985

A PATIENT SPIRIT, A RICH REWARD: CELLARING

Care, time, and luck: the three essential elements necessary for the keeping and serving of a fine wine. This last item, of course, is out of the hands of even the most faithful oenophile. But with sufficient time and care lavished on a wine, the role of luck may be played to a minimum.

The decanter has been one essential tool in the process of caring for fine wines. The glass bottle has been equally essential in modern wine storage. And for those with a collector's spirit (and a little patience), cellaring wine is another delightful way to improve and enjoy those bottles that will eventually grace the table.

"For several months after bottling, fine wines are often in a sort of state of dumb shock," writes wine authority Hugh Johnson. "They seem to sulk." For this reason, Johnson stores all fine wines for at least several months before sampling.

Everyday wine is typically ready to be consumed when it is bottled. That's why it's so easy to purchase a bottle and finish it in the same evening with a good degree of pleasure. Even some everyday reds will develop depth and class with just six months of storage, and fine wines will improve immeasurably. To take advantage of this potential for improvement, and to provide cherished friends and family with an extraordinary beverage and irreplaceable memories, consider creating a personal cellar.

But where should one store a lusty red? Ideally, in an ancient underground cave. Cool, dark, and somewhat humid, the earth remains the ideal cradle for a developing wine. But for those who are not so handy with the shovel, there are modern

A wine country cellar, such as this one in Sonoma County, is a safe home for aging wine.

alternatives. One needs only to choose a space and alter it to meet a few basic requirements: temperature, darkness, and humidity.

Any place that can be appropriately insulated can house wine. The temperature should hover around 50 degrees Fahrenheit, but anywhere between 45 and 64 degrees will do. The temperature should remain steady in order to prevent premature aging. A calm atmosphere, with no more than mild vibrations, is also ideal. As for light conditions, a cellar's darkness is not merely incidental; wines in clear- and tinted-glass bottles are as vulnerable to light as they are to temperature. Too much of either will age a wine prematurely. Finally, a cellar should be moderately humid. Humidity keeps cork pliable and fully expanded in the bottleneck. A humidifier may be helpful, but, more simply, a bowl of moist sand will do the job nearly as well.

Where are such conditions to be found? A bit of creativity will lend a range of options. Homeowners may hire a contractor to dig a small cellar under the garage or elsewhere on a property. If this seems a daunting proposition, then a small room or cupboard, insulated well, will also work, as will the inside of a blocked, unused chimney, or the bottom of a wardrobe, perhaps. Wine storage units, refrigerators made just for wine, are now readily available. And for the truly dedicated, a special room, insulated, air-conditioned, and dimmed, may be the perfect home for a promising new collection.

After all, it will be lovely to unearth that treasured bottle, bring it to its ideal serving temperature, and prepare to decant a wine that has been waiting, safely stored, for its moment of uncorking—its moment to shine.

Margrit and Robert Mondavi's private cellar features wooden racks for storing bottles horizontally.

An eighteenth-century antique bottle carrier.

An eighteenth-century antique padlocked bottle carrier.

A contemporary silver-wire wine cradle.

CHILLING WINE WITH STYLE

WINE COOLERS AND MONTEITHS

T'S SOMETHING WE SELDOM think of today, but chilling once held an esteemed place in the ritual of serving wines, white and red alike. In fact, from the sixteenth until the mid-nineteenth century, a host's dining room was simply incomplete without the proper equipment for lowering the temperature of wine. Naturally, artisans were not long in developing an assortment of stylish items expressly for this purpose.

The most impressive (and expensive) of these accoutrements was also the most straightforward in both design and name: the wine cooler. Often placed upon the floor to the side of the dining table, sitting low to the ground on clawed feet or perched atop wooden legs, wine coolers resembled exceedingly charming miniature bathtubs. The earliest versions were low, wide, and also quite large, since they were expected to hold multiple bottles during grand feasts; just before decanting, servants would pluck each bottle from the chilled water. These coolers were crafted of delicate brass and copper—unfortunate choices, as it turned out, since the oval bellies of these floor-bound vessels would inevitably suffer a kick or two during their tenure. Thus, it is no wonder that, as the years passed, hardier silver, marble, and mahogany—more durable than brass and copper—became the materials of choice.

Queen Victoria herself, one of history's most influential arbiters of style, had a grand silver wine cooler in her private dining room at Windsor Castle, reports a mysterious Countess X in 1904. The cooler "was considered perhaps the best example of

> *Glass wine-coolers, half filled with water, should be placed next to each person at table.*
>
> —CHARLES WILLIAM DAY,
> *Hints on Etiquette and the Usages of Society: With a Glance at Bad Habits,* 1844

Charles Meer Webb's 1883 painting A Satisfying Meal *depicts the use of wine coolers in centuries past.*

silver-work at Windsor," the countess writes. "It was a feature that struck all visitors as soon as they entered the apartment."

For George Washington, a silver wine cooler (also called a "cistern," the term for any wine cooler made from silver) became a peace offering, and a symbol of solidarity. When fellow politician Alexander Hamilton threatened to sink under the weight of a scandalous extramarital affair, Washington sent one such wine cooler to his friend, along with a letter: "Not for any intrinsic value the thing possesses, but as a token of my sincere regard and friendship for you and as a remembrance of me, I pray you to accept a wine cooler for four bottles," he writes, thus assuring Hamilton of his place in American political society. There were probably more valuable wine coolers made in the eighteenth century, but we can guess that none was more valued than this one.

A more diminutive but no less beautiful chilling device came into use during the eighteenth century and remained popular for 150 years. The tabletop wine cooler held one or two bottles of wine and was practical for intimate gatherings. Small enough to grace the table, its design featured handles for easy portability. In appearance it was akin to a vase: a graceful, curved object with rounded belly and sloping neck. In some cases the tabletop cooler resembled a bucket, with a cylindrical shape and straight sides. Early craftsmen tended to make these items in pairs, presumably to be placed at each end of a long dining table, or to add a symmetrical accent to a sideboard. In the late eighteenth century, porcelain models were somewhat popular. But, once again, silver took top billing, as it does today—for what material, other than glass, is more elegant?

Though glass tabletop coolers were used in the mid-nineteenth century, silver models have always been the standard.

A classic silver tabletop wine cooler and a decanter complement a well-stocked cellar.

These eighteenth-century English toleware monteiths were created in the French mode.

The modern host can easily find silver-plated replicas of beautiful antique wine coolers; acrylic chillers are also widely available. But, though these acrylic alternatives may be less costly and easier to find, they do come with some significant drawbacks. As wine writer Babs Harrison wisely points out, "Not only are they ugly today, they will be similarly ugly in the next century." The classics, on the other hand, always impress and forever endure.

Monteiths

Because seventeenth- and eighteenth-century diners preferred to chill their glasses as well as their wine, the monteith was always present at the most elegant tables. This glass-chilling device is said to be named for a seventeenth-century Scottish gentleman, James Monteith, who wore a cloak with a ridged hemline. The similarly scalloped rim of the monteith held ten to twelve glasses by their feet as their bowls were plunged into an oval or round cavity filled with cool, fresh water.

The French monteith, though it served the same purpose, was not called a monteith at all, but a *seau crénelé,* or crenulated bucket. However, a clunky tin pail the seau was most definitely not. No larger than a serving bowl, it graced the French table as part of an elegant dessert service. Thomas Jefferson, who was known for his love of France, wine, and French wines alike, had a most special set of seaux for his table. On each seau's waved sides of white porcelain, delicate gold flourishes were painted, and garlands of painted blue flowers adorned the scalloped rim. This pattern, known as *guirlandes de barbeaux,*

Antique monteiths, which were designed to chill wineglasses, are often used as centerpieces and are sought by many collectors.

*I have lived
temperately ...
I double the doctor's
recommendation of
a glass and a half of
wine a day and even
treble it with a friend.*

—THOMAS JEFFERSON,
Letter to Dr. Vine Utley, 1819

or cornflower garland, surely delighted Jefferson's guests—and so, we may imagine, did the story of its origin. First crafted by the peerless Sèvres porcelain factory and hand painted by Geneviève Le Roy Taillandier (the wife of a Sèvres craftsman), the seau that eventually chilled glasses at Monticello was actually made for none other than Louis XVI during the 1780s. Its royal pattern had adorned a dining room of the Palace of Versailles—the most lavish setting for wine since the Persian opulence described by John Chardin (see page 41). Jefferson's Sèvres porcelain seau is still on display for all to see at Monticello.

For the modern table, an antique seau or monteith—whether of silver, gilt-edged porcelain, pewter, brass, or toleware—makes a distinctive centerpiece. Chilling glasses may be out of vogue, but charm and history never are.

MODERN-DAY TECHNIQUES FOR CHILLING WINES

Today, of course, chilling is neither as rampant nor as extreme as it was in days past. No longer is it deemed necessary to chill red wine glasses, for example. But for wine to be fully appreciated and honored, it must still be served at its optimum temperature.

For most red and white wines, the ideal temperature for drinking is similar to the temperature for storage: between 50 and 60 degrees Fahrenheit. Many people utilize their refrigerators to chill white wines, but the average refrigerator temperature (44 degrees Fahrenheit) is actually too cold for most, and this manner of chilling wines takes quite a long time, since air is a poor conductor. Immersing a bottle in a cooler of icy water for eight minutes will bring the wine's temperature down by 10 degrees in a manner both more efficient and more tasteful. To bring the temperature up instead (which one may need to do if a red wine has been inadvertently stored in a refrigerator or other cold place), one simply fills the container with warm water.

White wines, expected to taste lighter and offer more refreshment, may be chilled to a cooler temperature than their red counterparts—but the difference is not as great as one might think. At the low end of the scale, a tart white may be served at a chilly 45 degrees Fahrenheit; a fine old Cabernet will do better at the high end, around 65 degrees Fahrenheit. Though it is often said that red wine should be served at "room temperature," it is also wise to remember that when this term was coined, before central heating had brought about a dramatic increase of the average home temperature, a typical dining room might have been as cold as 60 degrees Fahrenheit. Thus, despite the popular focus on chilling only white wines, a red wine at a warmer room temperature may in fact benefit from a few minutes' bath in a cooler of icy water.

The silver tabletop cooler, which allows for the subtle manipulation of a wine's temperature, still has an essential place in modern wine service. Such care lavished on a bottle of fine wine, bringing it to its optimal temperature before uncorking, will surely create an impression on one's guests. As a part of a careful, artful wine presentation, it will make a positive impression on one's wine as well.

This double wine cooler comes with sleeves to keep the bottles separated, making them easy to remove and replace—perfect for large gatherings.

PROTECTED FOR AGES, FREE IN A MOMENT

CORKS AND CORKSCREWS

A WINE'S UNCORKING IS A RELEASE

and an exposure, the triumphant (or disappointing) fruition of years—sometimes centuries—of slow and silent development. Like a debutante arriving at her ball, a wine about to be uncorked causes everyone to wonder, Will she present herself as an elegant, blossoming beauty, full of charm and character, or will she flop? In the case of a fine wine, only time will tell. One can only present it with care and hope for the best.

The cork's concept is simple: a plug that prevents an aging wine from escaping its bottle. Nothing has proven better at this simple task, for nothing can touch cork's combination of lightness, near impermeability, and elasticity. Its counterpart, the corkscrew, is equally uncomplicated but just as vital to the ritual of serving wine—for without it a matured wine would be forever trapped. It is interesting, then, to follow the development of the cork and corkscrew, and to learn how many centuries these essential implements waited to be invented, accepted, and finally given the attention they so richly deserve.

A cork's imprint reveals its origins: 1976 marked Jordan Winery's first vintage.

A HISTORY OF CORKS AND CORKSCREWS

For an object that performs its task so admirably, the cork has been woefully underrated. Corks from Portuguese cork oak trees have been available for sealing wine since the time of ancient Rome. There is even evidence that these early wine drinkers used cork to plug their amphorae during aging and

Cork, the standard for centuries, with its surrounding rituals, is now being challenged by new innovations.

transport. Is it possible, then, that the amphora's influence can be seen in yet another aspect of wine service (along with decanting and vessels)?

It *is* possible, and true—but in the development of the cork, the amphora's influence was actually quite negative. Examining the neck of one of these ancient vessels, one can easily understand why. Rough, uneven, and irregularly sized, the amphora's neck, made of pottery, was incredibly difficult to seal. A cork alone would not do it. Ancient corks were as irregular as the necks they sought to plug; cut from the bark face of the cork oak, they formed uneven circles that may or may not have fitted any particular amphora neck. The inadequacy of cork led the Romans to contrive a number of equally mediocre plugs, including pitch, clay, leaves and reeds, and cork coated with resin. Given what we know about the quality of ancient wines, we can guess that each of these options was as poor as the next. Even cork had not yet seen its glory day.

What changed everything was the glass bottle. Glass bottles forever improved the quality and character of wine, as well as the rituals of wine service; now let us look to its plug.

The cork, which is so commonplace today that we hardly think of it, may seem a small matter in the history of wine. Without it, though, what would the bottle be?

That question is easily answered. Without the cork to seal it, the glass bottle would be not significantly different from its cousin and counterpart, the glass decanter. As noted previously,

The cork and the silver stopper are both friends of the wine bottle—but only the cork will seal it for a lifetime.

Denis Diderot's engraving Manufacture of Bottle Corks, *circa 1770, illustrates how the modern cork came into being.*

Ground glass stoppers, no longer used to seal bottles, are still employed to close decanters.

even in the late seventeenth century, the early days of glass, these two items were not easily distinguishable from one another. Whether it was technically a decanter or a bottle, the glass vessel's preferred plug was not a cork but a stopper of ground glass.

Not surprisingly, the glass stopper did not long remain the favorite for bottles. For decanters, which do not need to be sealed tightly the way bottles do, a loose-fitting glass stopper worked perfectly well and still does, even to this day. However, when it came to bottles, the glass stopper had almost nothing (apart from its attractiveness) going for it. It was expensive, since it had to be designed and produced to fit individual bottlenecks (which surely caused trouble for manufacturers, as bottles were not yet regular in size and shape). Worse, once a stopper was sealed in place in the bottleneck, no device could easily remove it; the usual method of extraction was to break the bottle. As thrilling as this bottle smashing must have been, the cork seems a much more practical choice.

We now know the cork's true identity: humble, simple, and small, yet perfectly suited to its occupation. But, before the use of cork became widespread, seventeenth- and eighteenth-century wine drinkers saw the cork as something else: a traitor, not to be trusted. Once corks began to be used as wine bottle stoppers, it was thought—incorrectly—that a cork, once in the bottle, would secretly admit large quantities of air to ambush the wine inside. This misunderstanding was probably a result of cork's uneven quality in these early days of production; an imperfect cork might unwittingly lend the wine some of its own "corky" flavor. Corks improved over time, but their suspected misdeeds did not go easily from wine lovers' memories.

As late as 1825, bottlers at the renowned Château Lafite were still stoppering their valued vintages with glass.

Corks were at the center of another controversy at the turn of the twentieth century, a time when French wineries did not yet bottle wines on site. Dishonest dealers had been taking advantage of this situation by using false labels to trick consumers into purchasing second-rate wines at first-rate prices. The wineries decided to combat this problem by printing the winery name and vintage on the cork, thus increasing the cork's significance in the eyes of both the sommelier and the wine drinker.

Over the years, the embattled cork gradually proved its loyalty and won the position it was destined to assume: friend of the bottle, enemy of the air, and trusted protector of wines.

Pulling a cork always has a touch of drama about it.

—HUGH JOHNSON,
How to Enjoy Wine, 1985

If such a thing is possible, the corkscrew's history is even more mysterious than that of the cork. Extraordinarily little is known about the corkscrew's invention and early use. We can assume that it originated with the cork itself—for how else would a cork be extracted? But, if the truth be told, as is the case with most matters related to the corkscrew, no one really knows.

A few facts have emerged from the corkscrew's murky history. The first printed mention of this device came in 1681, describing it as "a steel worm [a device employed by contemporary gunsmiths to remove wadding and bullets from the barrels of guns] used for the drawing of corks out of bottles." We know, too, that the term "bottlescrew" remained in vogue

Regardless of the material it is made from, the T-bar corkscrew, such as this scrimshaw model, remains an incredibly useful object.

until 1720, when "corkscrew" was finally coined. Most other information that we have about the development of the corkscrew has been gleaned from the devices themselves.

Over the centuries, the three elements of the T-bar style corkscrew—the screw, the handle, and the shaft—have remained constant. Within this basic structure, though, corkscrews changed in size and shape, growing ornamentation that was sometimes lavish, sometimes whimsical. Some corkscrews were made of steel, others bronze or silver, and still others mahogany and walnut. Engravings adorned many. Antlers appeared as handles, as did boar's tusk and buffalo horn. The "Thomason's screw," patented by Edward Thomason in 1802, featured a metal barrel to cover the screw and a brush to clean the bottle mouth. A few years later, the "King's screw" added a second handle.

Despite its many incarnations and various adornments, the corkscrew remains a humble object. Its only goal is to do its job well: to remove the cork (in one piece, ideally) and to release the wine, with all of its time-won pleasures.

UNCORKING WITH STYLE

The act of removing a cork is as simple as the cork itself. When the wine is brought to the table, it should stand upright. With a gentle touch, the host uses a knife to cut off the upper portion of the foil capsule, revealing the top of the cork. He then wipes the area with a clean cloth and smoothly extracts the cork with his preferred corkscrew, without jarring the bottle. The

A circle of corkscrews includes King's and Thomason's screws.

It is obvious that very soon after the use of cork was introduced, the corkscrew must have been introduced: otherwise the glass bottle would not have been the restful home of the wine, but its lifelong prison.

—ANDRÉ L. SIMON,
Bottlescrew Days, 1927

trick is to release the cork with care and finesse, maintaining the delicacy of the process and the elegance of the table.

Like all things, the grand uncorking may not come off as grandly or easily as one hopes. Occasionally the cork may break, leaving a portion to blockade the bottleneck. To counter this problem, the host may reinsert the corkscrew at an angle, pushing the remaining cork against the neck while slowly pulling it out. If this technique is unsuccessful, then the host may push the cork all the way in and use a three-pronged wire device, or "claw," to take out the floating cork bits.

The cork, once removed from the bottleneck, can tell an attentive server much about the wine with which it has kept such close quarters. First, he examines the cork's appearance. If the cork is stained with a deep color, then the wine is likely older, tannic, and full bodied; if the cork appears untouched, then the wine may be younger or lighter. It is also essential to feel the cork for moistness. A dry cork may mean that the wine has been stored upright, a method that has been appropriately out of mode since the seventeenth century, and a dry, shrunken cork may signify the oxidation of an aging wine. Finally, the server will wish to smell the cork. Beware a moldy odor, Hugh Johnson cautions, which may indicate that the wine is "corked" (or tainted by TCA, a combination of mold and other unsavory elements) and thus undrinkable. If all is well with the cork, however, then one can feel confident in moving on to the next delightful steps of wine service: decanting, pouring, tasting, and indulging in a wonderful, well-formed wine.

Today, we enjoy the ideal combination: bottle, cork, corkscrew, decanter. They have worked together for centuries

A cork's aroma offers wine director Shelley Lindgren many clues to a wine's taste and quality.

Here's to the corkscrew—a useful key to unlock the storehouse of wit, the treasury of laughter, the front door of fellowship, and the gate of pleasant folly.

—W.E.P. FRENCH,
from the wine list of
Commander's Palace in New
Orleans, courtesy of John
McDonald, Dallas

now, and it appears that those who treasure fine wine may rest easy, the tools of the traditions having been finally found, accepted, and perfected.

In seeming contradiction, the cork enjoys no such leisure. Once again, its loyalty and ability are in question, and a manufactured item is poised to take its place. With TCA threatening the quality of cork, the world of wine now prepares itself (with some nervousness) for the encroachment of the screw cap and the synthetic cork.

The popularity of the screw cap is not hard to explain: The natural character of cork brings with it some variability in quality, and the screw cap (because it is constructed of aluminum alloy, tin foil, and other such materials) carries none of these concerns. While the cork is inserted deep into the bottleneck like a plug, the screw cap acts more like a seal, hugging the outside of the neck. Some say the cork may allow taint from gas, air, or its own material; the screw cap, apparently, will do no such thing.

Synthetic corks were developed in the 1990s in response to rising natural cork prices. However, when dealing with a treasured wine, one finds that the least expensive option is not necessarily the best. These manufactured closures are considered acceptable for wines that are bottled for five years or less. When they are colored neon purple or cobalt blue, though, *acceptable* is not the word that comes to mind.

Not surprisingly, a movement is under way among traditionalists to preserve the cork, for it has done well by wines during its centuries of service. What is lost in abandoning the cork to the modern screw cap? First, of course, the corkscrew, and the ritual of uncorking described above. Next, the time-tested ability to assist in the proper aging of a wine (screw caps have not yet been proven to do this job well). The cork, a product of the natural world, has sealed innumerable precious wines and allowed subtle changes in these wines over time. And, as is possible only through the vast changeability of nature, it has helped to create an atmosphere of exciting uncertainty, in which one cannot expressly determine how any particular bottle of wine will live out its life. Will it succeed or fail? How will this year's sun affect next year's wine? How will the soil change, and the rain? How much air will sneak in through a cork's pores to intermingle with the aging wine, and what miraculous results will occur when these elements mix?

The cork is a natural thing, like wine itself. And, like wine, it may be somewhat unpredictable. Like wine, it may even, from time to time, fail us. But when it succeeds, when the elements of nature come together to produce something more wonderful than humans alone could ever have imagined or engineered, then we may only be grateful, and wait to see what wondrous things nature will bring to our wineglasses . . . next year.

A whimsical take on the classic corkscrew.

Your heart will rise on the wine as light as a cork.

—ALEXANDRE DUMAS,
The Romances of Alexandre Dumas, 1898

AN ELEGANT DISPLAY

WINEGLASSES

ℒIKE THE CORK, THE DECANTER, AND

so many of the accoutrements of wine presentation, wineglasses deserve to be admired—for their beauty or simplicity, yes, but also because they can contribute so greatly to the experience of tasting a fine wine.

Baccarat's modern crystal wineglass, from the Oenologie collection, is simple and perfectly designed for its intended use.

𝒜N OBJECT OF ART: THE WINEGLASS

The ideal wineglass is shaped, sized, and crafted not only to hold its wine but also to display it in the best possible manner. Although artfully shaped glasses bring out the best in particular varietals, some glass qualities are universal. For any wine, the glass should be ample enough to hold a quarter of a liter of liquid but not be excessively large, and it should taper inward at the rim. This subtle manipulation of shape helps to concentrate the aromas and draw them up toward the nose. On the best wineglasses, the lip is smooth, not rolled—a detail that may seem inconsequential but can make all the difference in tasting. Drunk from a glass with a smooth lip, the wine runs directly over the tip of the tongue, where one tastes sweetness; by contrast, if sipped from a rolled-lip glass, the same wine is likely to bypass the tip of the tongue and splash upon other, less-desirable tasting zones. The stem is important as well—it should be slender and tall, with a sufficient foot.

Georg Riedel, who represents the tenth generation in his family's world-renowned wineglass firm, discovered that the

These antique wineglasses are part of Margrit and Robert Mondavi's private wine collection.

*Wine to me is passion.
It's family and friends.
It's warmth of heart
and generosity of spirit.
. . . It's the essence of
civilization and the
art of living.*

—ROBERT MONDAVI,
*Harvests of Joy: How the Good Life
Became Great Business,* 1998

content commands the shape: "The delivery of a wine's 'message,' its bouquet and taste, depend on the form of the glass. It is the responsibility of a glass to convey the wine's messages in the best manner to the human senses."

Red wines flourish in a glass with a round or oval bowl tapering inward at the rim. The glass should be large enough to deliver oxygen to the wine and display the wine's rich color and aroma when half full. White wine, however, prefers a more-elongated oval bowl, also tapering inward at the rim. These are the basics, the essentials in any collection. Other specialty glasses, such as those for Champagne, Riesling, Burgundy, sherry, port, and dessert wines, are also widely available and make fun accents for service and display. Baccarat's extensive collection, represented on pages 82–83, includes almost every modern shape one can imagine.

Over time, wine has been poured into earthenware, stone-ware, pewter, and numerous other materials, but only crystal has achieved the degree of perfection necessary to do justice to a great wine. Though the Georgian and Victorian eras sparkled with elaborate glass vessels—solid balusters, lighter balustroids with air twist stems, stippled goblets, multitoned glasses—simple, faultless crystal ultimately prevailed, and it remains the standard even now. Thus, the drink itself, and not elaborate ornamentation, is what attracts the eye.

Wine Presentation and Enjoyment

The simplicity of crystal reigns today, along with a simplicity of service; for this we may be grateful. Like wineglasses themselves, their presentation rituals were once incredibly complex.

Woe to be a young hostess serving wine in nineteenth- and early-twentieth-century society. The decanter, the glass bottle, the cork, and the wineglass had all finally come together, and wine now had its chance to be perfectly served. However, never before or since has the choreography of the table been more severely structured, or more closely observed. For those brave souls who would attempt the feat of holding a dinner party, an army of etiquette arbiters awaited—each with a seemingly endless list of rules, and fresh expressions of horror at the ready, should one of these standards go unmet.

"The [wine] bottle goes down the left side and up the right, and the same bottle never passes twice," advises an anonymous "Gentleman" in his 1836 *Laws of Etiquette*. "If you do not drink, always pass the bottle to your neighbour."

Society hostess Ms. Agnes H. Morton, gentle but firm, heaps instruction and yet more instruction upon the hostess in 1909. On serving: "Everything at table is handed at the left, *except wine*, which is offered at the right." And on settings: "A glass goblet for water is set at the right, about eight inches from the edge of the table; if wine is to be served the requisite glasses are grouped about the water goblet."

This modern Murano wineglass was inspired by an antique.

This Argos wineglass was created by French glassmaker Lalique.

Pages 82–83: Baccarat's crystal wineglass collection, shown here in part, features a shape for every wine type.

Perfection

Montaigne

Clara

Masséna

Brummel

Monaco

Oenologie

Parme

Rohan

Sévigné

Mille Nuits

Filao

Onde

Stream

Vence

Véga

Capri

Harcourt

Dom Pérignon

Saint Rémy

Epicure

Maladetta

Arcade

Neptune

Narcisse

Impérator

Rivoli

Concorde

Byzance

Empire

What a beautiful object the wineglass is! It holds the wine and also offers it, a trap and a display case at the same time.

—EMILE PEYNAUD,
The Taste of Wine, 1996

Even a mischievously funny Benjamin Franklin has strong views on the subject of serving wine: "Do not then offer water except to children," he writes. "'Tis a mistaken piece of politeness, and often very inconvenient."

By 1910, a multitude of opinions swirled around the subject of serving wine. Today, thank goodness, the opinions have been harnessed, the rules simplified. What matters most is the wine, and its safe journey from the decanter to each guest's waiting glass.

Some rules do persist, however. When serving wine informally at home, it is considered proper to set the wineglasses to the right of each guest—a sensible enough practice, since the majority of people are right handed, and it should never be difficult to reach one's wine.

A colored crystal wineglass, Tommy by St. Louis, recalls an earlier style.

When pouring wine formally, as in a restaurant, the host walks around the table with the decanter, filling each glass from the right side of each guest. Women are served first; the host serves himself last. To avoid spills, he leaves each glass flat on the table and brings the decanter to the glass, pouring slowly. Considering the generously sized bowls of modern wineglasses (which are much larger than those of vintage glasses), it is best to fill them halfway at most. At the end of the pour, he gently twists the decanter to stop any drips. It is wise to keep a napkin on hand as well, so as to preserve that which is nearly impossible to retrieve once it is gone—the pure white linen of the tablecloth.

In a less formal setting, where guests may prefer to serve themselves, the host merely passes the decanter around the table. Tradition dictates that guests pass to the left, since presumably it is easier to receive the decanter with one's right hand. The direction one passes the decanter should not overly concern the host, of course. One must only ensure that every guest has the opportunity to fill his or her glass and enjoy the party.

Even one of the strictest etiquette advisers mentioned above, Agnes H. Morton, agrees with this simple tenet. "Remember, first of all, to give *yourself* to your guest," she writes. "Then, if he is appreciative, he will not criticise your simple dinner, nor grumble at the flavor of your wine."

This wineglass, Trianon by St. Louis, is well etched with diamonds, panels, and steps.

The trumpet-bowl wineglass,
like this Maharani glass
by Moser, has been popular since
the mid-eighteenth century.

AN ELEGANT RITUAL: TOASTING

Just one step remains before the first sip of wine is taken—before experiencing the eagerly anticipated pleasure of that first taste—and it requires nothing more than a full glass and a full heart. The act of toasting, which has persisted in some form since the time of the ancients, allows the host or his guests to express the goodwill inspired by the gathering, the meal, and the drink.

The host may wish to make the first toast, welcoming his guests and inviting them to enjoy the meal to be served. He stands and, with a clean knife or fork, taps lightly upon a glass to call for his guests' attention. Then, as he and his guests raise their glasses around the table, he speaks. Short and sweet speeches are to be desired; rambling is not (which is perhaps why the toast is best given early in the evening, rather than after a few bottles have been enjoyed). When the speech is concluded, guests clink their glasses or simply drink, depending on the space at the table and the occasion; if a clink is easily accomplished, then it's quite appropriate, but not if guests must climb over the table in an effort to reach the next glass. What is important is that the sentiment of the speech be acknowledged.

With a special toast, a suitably and elegantly shaped wineglass, and a group of appreciative friends, the wine experience becomes truly personal, not only a ritual performed throughout history but a tradition to practice at one's own table—and a pleasurable prelude to the first taste.

Albert-August Fourie depicts the elegant ritual of toasting in his 1886 painting
The Wedding Meal at Yport.

THE GREATEST PLEASURE

TASTING AND
APPRECIATING WINES

T IS NO WONDER

that crystal-clear glasses have become the modern standard: They welcome the eye, inviting one to appreciate the liquid depths of red or gold. Before a fine wine is ever tasted, its appearance can convey to one with a trained eye the wine's variety, age, and sometimes even the vintage and texture, too. However, although the rituals of uncorking, decanting, pouring, and observing a wine do offer clues to how that wine will taste and feel, its true nature is never completely revealed until it is tasted.

Eighty percent of wine appreciation is in the aroma and bouquet of the wine.

—ROB DAVIS,
Winemaker,
Jordan Vineyard & Winery,
Healdsburg, California

TASTING WINE: A PRIMER

Any wine aficionado will agree: the first taste is a moment best savored slowly. The glass, filled halfway with well-decanted wine, sits upon the table. Keeping the glass on the flat surface, the taster first places several fingers on the glass's foot and rotates the glass in gentle circles. This circling motion increases evaporation and thus intensifies the wine's aroma, so one should then lift the glass, tilt it toward the nose, and enjoy.

It is important to maintain an even breathing rhythm and smell by inhaling slowly, never by sniffing. Two or three measured inhalations should suffice to reveal all of the layers of the bouquet, which will emerge from the wine in succession. In most cases, the circling of the glass will release pleasant odors; however, it may have quite the opposite effect, depending

"The nose of wine is a very didactic tool," says winemaker Maurizio Castelli.

Checking the aroma and the bouquet of the wine.

upon the condition of the wine. Be wary of wines that emit the smell of burnt matches (indicating an excess of sulfur), mold, or mustiness. As is the case with the cork, some wine experts rely almost entirely upon the nose to determine the quality of a particular bottle. After all, a wine that offends a taster's nose will surely do no better for the mouth.

Of course, nothing compares to the pleasure of drawing a fine wine onto one's palate, tasting the depth of its flavors, and feeling it glide down the throat. For this most basic experience, simply taking a sip is enough. But to truly appreciate a wine, to sense the subtle nuances of age and flavor, employing a bit of care and control can transform the experience into a memorable, informative one. Below is one such method of tasting wine, as recommended by wine expert Emile Peynaud.

The taster first lifts the glass and tilts it toward his lips, the rim of the glass resting on the bottom lip. The sip of wine touches the tip of his tongue and then flows over it. Now, he allows the wine to flow back into his mouth. At this point, a practice known as "chewing" begins, in which he gently moves the wine around his mouth. The tongue should gently manipulate the wine and press it against the roof of the mouth. He makes a series of small swallows during this process. Thus the wine's flavors and texture are fully absorbed and appreciated.

When the wine is at its best, one will sense a delicious balance of fruit, alcohol, acidity, and sweetness—the four basic elements of a wine's flavors. As any wine lover will attest, there are innumerable other tastes to be discovered in any given bottle. In the layers of a fine wine, one may sense green apples and ripe blackberries, rich earth and wet stones, tart currant and flower petals, rich gorgonzola and smoky hazelnut. Vanilla may linger—so may cherry, walnut, pineapple, graham cracker, cedar, mint, and countless other flavors. Some barrel-aged wines may have an oaky taste, which can be interesting as long as it doesn't overpower the wine's other flavors. Similarly, the taste of a red wine may be influenced by its tannin (the substance found in the skins and stems of grapes that can make one's gums feel rough and dry). Extremely useful in aging red wines, tannin does not usually present a problem; however, like oak, it should never be so strong as to overwhelm.

The term "off-ness," untechnical though it may be, has become popular among wine aficionados to describe the negative quality of a wine that has, appropriately enough, gone off. And, unfortunately for all, a wine has nearly as many ways to go off, or wrong, as it does to go right. The tasting ritual is the only sure way to identify and banish such a wine before it sours a sumptuous meal. This may support some experts' claims that it is preferable to decant a wine before guests are gathered; that way, one can be assured of the wine's quality oneself. Alternatively, after decanting one may invite guests to share in the tasting process, or use a *tastevin* device, a personal tasting vessel.

The wide, gleaming silver bowl of the tastevin, used by French wine merchants to sample new vintages in candlelit cellars since the fifteenth century, is able to catch even the dimmest light—and in it, a red wine's color and clarity shows more vividly than it does in wood or glass. A particularly ingenious version of the tastevin is the *tasses jumelles*. A hinged set of cups that close like a compact to fit snugly into one's pocket,

cedar

vanilla

chocolate

blackberries

cherries

coffee beans

blueberries

violets

this is a wonderful tool for comparing two different wines. Today, both devices are used mainly in fine restaurants. Equally useful in homes as well, they may assist a host in conducting a discreet tasting before serving a wine—a wise move if one suspects a particular wine may be "off."

What are the ways a wine can go wrong? A fairly mild offense is a lack of balance, which may be characterized by too much acidity, oak, tannin, or alcohol. A slightly more troublesome problem is mustiness, a quality that brings to mind "an attic that nobody goes into," advise wine writers Robert Joseph and Margaret Rand; such an odor and taste may be a sign of oxidation or bacterial infection from a dirty barrel. This same mustiness may instead signal "corkiness," which arises when the cork or wine is infected by TCA (see page 72). Worst of all, a sour taste is a not-too-subtle indication that the wine has begun to turn to vinegar.

Along with the smell and the taste, the texture, or "mouthfeel," is important in judging a wine. The experienced oenophile will note whether the wine feels rich and syrupy or water thin.

The raised center of this seventeenth-century-style silver "ombelic" tastevin affords an excellent view of the wine's color.

A set of eighteenth-century French tastevins.

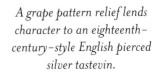

A grape pattern relief lends character to an eighteenth-century-style English pierced silver tastevin.

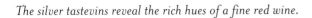

The silver tastevins reveal the rich hues of a fine red wine.

In water one sees one's own face; but in wine, one beholds the heart of another.

—FRENCH PROVERB

Part of the fun in enjoying an older vintage is to witness a wine evolve in the glass.

—SHELLEY LINDGREN,
Wine Director and
General Manager, A16 restaurant,
San Francisco

If it has good texture, it should also have good structure, firm like a tea or soda. Additionally, liquid that clings to the sides of the glass, leaving "legs," indicates that the wine is likely thick and concentrated. If it looks and acts thin, then it likely tastes and feels that way, too. The finish conveys information about the quality of a wine as well. Flavors of a mediocre wine will fade quickly; those of an exceptional wine will linger.

Most simply, every wine should please the senses. If a wine does not meet this standard, then it is entirely appropriate to reject it for a new bottle. In a restaurant, a diner may politely announce the problem to the sommelier or waiter. A competent server will taste the wine and, upon confirming the fault, promptly bring a new bottle to the table. The private host, upon tasting an "off" wine, will calmly produce a new bottle from the cellar. Guests will surely forgive and forget most anything, as long as there is another bottle on hand.

With luck, however, the host will not find himself begging for forgiveness after properly chilling, uncorking, decanting, and pouring a fine wine. The tasting process, in which the wine's bouquet and flavors are finally engaged with the human senses, will delight guest and host alike.

From the taste of the wine poured into waiting glasses, to the warmth of the candlelight, to the flavors of the meal, the details are what come together to create a sumptuous, relaxing atmosphere.

A closer look at a red wine offers hints regarding taste and texture.

BEYOND BASIC

FURNISHINGS FOR FINE WINES

IN CENTURIES PAST,

when a dinner party was a carefully choreographed performance of refinement and service executed by a butler and his staff, a proper dining room required more than just a table and chairs.

> *Wine-service related furniture adds an element of surprise to any environment.*
>
> —HELGA HORNER,
> Interior Designer,
> Helga Horner Inc.

EARLY FURNISHINGS FOR WINE SERVICE

As early as the Middle Ages, the presentation of wine involved not only a squadron of servants but also specialized furniture. The aumbry was the most important item, providing a tableside stage for preparing both food and drink. The butler, who was charged with decanting and spicing wines, established his station here. From the aumbry, he sent the cupbearer to the table with fresh, full cups; he also received and refilled empty ones and oversaw all aspects of wine service.

In later centuries, the aumbry evolved into the side table, which also stood to the side of the dining table. A prelude to the sideboard, the side table was a new incarnation of a servants' workstation, still functional but now beautifully (and sometimes lavishly) crafted to suit the style of the increasingly elegant dining room. In some seventeenth- and eighteenth-century models, complex moldings disguise drawers for napkins, corkscrews, and other serving tools, and the marble top provides a lovely—and durable—space for rinsing and filling glasses. Some artisans of the time kept both practicality and the needs of the servants in mind, fitting tables with raised lips to

The sideboard, depicted in Joseph Benwell Clark's 1885 painting The Bachelor's Breakfast Table, *is equipped with everything necessary for serving.*

A corner console table transforms easily into a rafraichissoir.

contain any spilled wine. Such a design element was a thoughtful accommodation for the hardworking servants, who were expected to collect, fill, and return guests' glasses, all with ease and grace.

On certain occasions, however, it was the fashion for eighteenth-century male guests to serve themselves—an exclusive practice that led to the development of the wine table. After dinner, with the ladies ushered safely out of earshot, the men would gather near small mahogany tables to create a scene similar to that of the Greek symposium: wine, relaxation, and all manner of bawdy talk. The tables, with space for glasses and decanters, were stocked by servants ahead of time—that way, the men could enjoy absolute after-dinner privacy. Some more interesting models feature a superstructure with rounded holes meant to hold decanters, as well as fretted, or slotted, edges from which hung as many as twelve glasses at once.

Another type of wine table, which renowned furniture maker George Hepplewhite described in 1793 as the "Gentleman's Social Table," had a flat surface with deep, metal-lined, cylindrical holes for bottles or decanters. Few examples of these tables, also called *rafraichissoirs,* were seen after 1850, but recent modern interpretations of this style make clear why they were once so popular: with a flat mahogany surface for glasses and built-in containers for chilling bottles or decanters, the wine table offers at once beauty and functionality.

Today, wine tables provide space on which party guests can rest their glasses. Reproductions, though somewhat shorter than the grand eighteenth-century originals, are widely available and may be the perfect centerpiece for a lively twenty-first-century party.

THE SIDEBOARD: AN OBJECT OF UTILITY AND BEAUTY

Finally, from the various tables and trays that paraded through the dining rooms of the eighteenth and nineteenth centuries arose the often massive, usually functional, and always impressive sideboard. When imagining a sideboard, one generally thinks of rich, sturdy mahogany, since this has always been the material preferred by their makers. However, they do vary in decor and shape. Some sideboards, for example, often feature a serpentine shape—a protruding front that forms an elegant S-curve. Later models are boxier, with cubed units flanking a

A Louis XVI–style rafraichissoir is ideal for small spaces.

With a brass gallery framing an inset marble top, this Louis XIV–style cherry wood rafraichissoir is both graceful and functional.

A Louis XVI—style mahogany and faux porphyry petit occasional table in the manner of Riesener, with a swivel top, reveals a generously sized rafraichissoir pail.

simply drawn flat table. Still others were elaborately adorned with so many golden, neoclassical loops and swirls that it is hard to believe they were ever put to use. However, in the eighteenth and nineteenth centuries, most sideboards were used, and used well. For most were equipped with everything necessary for serving wine and food: drawers to store accessories, cupboards with hot coals to heat plates, wine coolers and cellarettes to chill wine, basins and urns for rinsing glasses and silver, slots for cutlery, and a broad surface on which to work.

Until as late as the turn of the twentieth century, everyone who was anyone had a sideboard. One reason for its increasing popularity: a new dining tradition known as *service à la russe.* Unlike *service à la française,* which deemed that serving dishes be set out upon the table, service à la russe dictated that food be plated before it was brought to the table, and that each guest be served a prepared plate. The sideboard then became quite helpful in the process of plating—and, as always, in the process of decanting wine.

Like the decanter, in the eighteenth and nineteenth centuries the sideboard was considered so essential, so de rigueur, that it was hardly remarked upon; however, like the decanter, it lingers in the background of novels and plays and etiquette books of this period. Sideboards furnish the dining rooms imagined by writers Charles Dickens, Washington Irving, Jonathan Swift, and Rudyard Kipling. Honoré de Balzac mentions them, as do Robert Louis Stevenson and Alexandre Dumas. But perhaps the best proof of the sideboard's importance comes from the United States government, whose War Department in 1903 listed the sideboard as a necessary item, along with beds and chairs and dining tables, to be provided for the homes of its married soldiers.

In today's era of self-service, the sideboard may be no more than a grand conversation piece, a convenient place to set serving platters, a mahogany presence that one always seems to be skirting on the way to the kitchen. Yet the sideboard retains its place in a formal dining room. Regard a beautiful antique sideboard as a testament to refined quality, a hallmark of tradition, an elegant grandfather reminding us of a time that was infinitely simpler—perhaps not in its serving and dining accoutrements and etiquette, but surely in its pleasures. These are timeless pleasures we may still enjoy today: wine, food, and the elegant alliance they form, an alliance we honor every time we dine with family and friends over a decanter of well-chosen wine. For it is through this unique alliance that we are able to share all—wine and food and our best hospitality—with those we treasure most.

Eighteenth-century French-style wine harvest tilt-top table.

The wine table is a conversation piece, and is also very versatile.

—JOHN KOZUBAL,
Wine Educator,
Jordan Vineyard & Winery,
Healdsburg, California

FROM THE VINEYARD TO THE TABLE

A VINTNER'S DINNER

A FINE WINE IS A BEAUTIFUL THING,

> *Sharing food and wine is really about friendship and conviviality, and living life to the fullest.*
>
> —TOM JORDAN,
> Founder,
> Jordan Vineyard & Winery,
> Healdsburg, California

and one that is meant to be shared. The rituals of decanting, from cellaring to tasting, both enhance the wine experience and provide unparalleled pleasure to the wine lover. However, the wine is but one part of what may be called high entertaining: pairing each bottle with a delicious dish, gathering around the table, and sharing food and wine with the people we care about most are the elements that transform an ordinary dining experience into a true celebration of life.

The recipes and wine recommendations that follow have been thoughtfully crafted by the Jordan Estate's own executive chef, Udo Nechutnys, whose inventive creations have delighted many of the Estate's treasured guests. Inspired by the flavors of the Northern California wine country, this chef's menu is a sumptuous study in the art of counterpoint: sweet and savory, rich and light, and spice and smoothness all play upon each other in a cascade of flavors. When paired with the right wines, these dishes sing: from the Roasted Sweet Onions with Chanterelle Mushrooms and Shallot-Herb Butter served with a crisp, fruity Chardonnay, to the Coq au Vin de Sonoma, Macaroni, et Champignons complemented by a full, multilayered Cabernet, each course is designed to delight the senses.

The wine is selected, the menu prepared. Now good friends and family may gather around the table, decant the first bottle, serve the first course, and share the first taste. Nothing could be more wonderful.

Friends gather over food and wine in a Jordan Estate dining room.

 VINTNER'S DINNER

Amuse-Bouche

Sparkling Wine

Roasted Sweet Onions with Chanterelle Mushrooms and Shallot-Herb Butter

2004 Jordan Chardonnay

Coq au Vin de Sonoma, Macaroni, et Champignons

2002 Jordan Cabernet Sauvignon

Cowgirl Creamery's Mt. Tam, Parmigiano-Reggiano, and Sonoma Dry Jack

1995 Jordan Cabernet Sauvignon

Hot Chocolate Cakes with Strawberry Salad

Beaume de Venise, Muscat

Amuse-Bouche

BeauSoleil Oysters with Ponzu Sauce.

The meal begins with a tasty *amuse-bouche*. Served alongside a crisp, fruity white wine, such as a Sparkling Wine, and drizzled with lemony ponzu sauce, BeauSoleil oysters from Canada pleasantly awaken the palate.

Roasted Sweet Onions with Chanterelle Mushrooms and Shallot-Herb Butter

A perfect first course for company, this dish mingles the sweetness of roasted onions with the earthiness of wild chanterelles. The onions are first cooked and then stuffed with the mushrooms, which have been sautéed and tossed with a flavored butter. The Alexander Valley Chardonnay, a crisp white with hints of citrus and apple, will nicely enhance the bold and subtle flavors of the dish.

Trim away any roots still attached to the onions, being careful to leave their skins intact.

Place the onions on a steamer rack over medium heat, cover the steamer, and steam until the onions are easily pierced to the core with a knife, about 50 minutes. Remove the onions to a plate and let cool.

Preheat the oven to 350 degrees F. Oil an ovenproof sauté pan large enough to accommodate the onions in a single layer.

Press down lightly on the top of each onion to create a flat base. Using a sharp knife, carefully slice off the top one-fifth of each onion and set aside to use as a

continued

FOR THE ONIONS:

8 small sweet onions such as Vidalia or Maui

8 tablespoons (½ cup) Chardonnay

8 tablespoons (½ cup) extra-virgin olive oil

8 teaspoons kosher salt

Freshly ground black pepper

FOR THE MUSHROOMS:

4 tablespoons (¼ cup) extra-virgin olive oil

1 ¼ pounds chanterelles, trimmed, brushed clean, and peeled

½ cup Shallot-Herb Butter (recipe follows)

Salt and freshly ground black pepper

Oysters with Ponzu Sauce

cap. With a paring knife, remove the 3 innermost segments from each onion to form a small recess for the mushrooms. Place 1 tablespoon of the Chardonnay, 1 tablespoon of the olive oil, 1 teaspoon of the kosher salt, and 2 turns of a pepper mill in each recess. Replace the onion tops, and place the onions in the prepared sauté pan.

Place the pan on the lowest oven rack and roast the onions until they are a rich brown and heated through, 20 to 30 minutes. Remove from the oven and tent loosely with aluminum foil to keep warm.

Just before the onions have finished roasting, cook the mushrooms: In a large sauté pan, heat the olive oil. Add the chanterelles and sauté until they have released their liquid, about 5 minutes. Add the Shallot-Herb Butter, season with a little salt and pepper, and toss to coat the mushrooms evenly.

Spoon the chanterelles into the warm onions and place the onions on individual plates. Replace the onion tops and serve immediately.

Serves 8

SHALLOT-HERB BUTTER

In a food processor, combine 1 cup (8 ounces) room-temperature unsalted butter, 1/4 cup minced shallot, 2 tablespoons minced garlic, 2 1/2 tablespoons minced fresh parsley, 2 tablespoons minced fresh chervil, and 1 1/2 tablespoons kosher salt. Pulse until the ingredients are evenly combined and the butter is a uniform green. Store the leftover butter in a tightly sealed container in the freezer for up to 2 months. Makes about 1 1/2 cups.

> *There are few pleasures as sensually exhilarating as sipping good wine and eating good food. When all of one's senses have been lit with the fire of an exceptional meal, one realizes the true meaning of the finer things in life.*
>
> —UDO NECHUTNYS,
> Executive Chef,
> Jordan Vineyard & Winery,
> Healdsburg, California

Roasted Sweet Onions with Chanterelle Mushrooms and Shallot-Herb Butter

FOR THE COQ AU VIN:

2 whole chickens, each 3½ to 4 pounds

1 pound carrots, trimmed and each cut into 2 or 3 pieces

5 onions, peeled and halved through the stem end

1 head garlic, separated into cloves and peeled

3 tablespoons chopped fresh parsley

3 tablespoons chopped fresh thyme

3 tablespoons chopped fresh marjoram

3 bay leaves

½ cup marc de Bourgogne

2 bottles (750 ml each) Cabernet Sauvignon

Salt and freshly ground black pepper

½ cup all-purpose flour

¾ cup extra-virgin olive oil

1 tablespoon unsweetened cocoa powder

1 pound white mushrooms, trimmed, brushed clean, and quartered

12 ounces macaroni

Chopped fresh parsley for garnish

Coq au Vin de Sonoma, Macaroni, et Champignons

This classic French dish likely originated as a peasant stew made with a tough, aged rooster (*coq*), since only the wealthy could regularly afford more tender fare. Today this simple, satisfying stew is typically made by braising chicken pieces, vegetables, and herbs (and often bacon or other cured pork) in a hearty red wine, making it an ideal dish to pair with an opulent, multi-layered red like the 2002 Jordan Cabernet Sauvignon.

Cut each chicken into 8 serving pieces. In a large bowl or other large nonreactive vessel, combine the chicken pieces, carrots, onions, and garlic. Add the parsley, thyme, marjoram, and bay leaves, and pour in the marc de Bourgogne and the wine. Season with a little salt and pepper and stir until combined evenly. Cover and marinate in the refrigerator for 48 hours.

Remove the chicken pieces from the marinade, drain well, and pat dry with paper towels. Reserve the marinade. Spread the flour on a large plate. One at a time, roll each chicken piece in the flour, coating evenly and tapping off the excess. In a large Dutch oven or other large ovenproof pot with a lid, heat the olive oil over medium heat. Working in batches to avoid crowding, brown the chicken pieces well on all sides, about 10 minutes for each batch. Using a slotted spoon, transfer the chicken to a rack or paper towels to drain. Set the Dutch oven with its remaining oil aside.

Preheat the oven to 325 degrees F. Scoop the vegetables out of the marinade and set them aside in a colander to drain. Pour the marinade into a saucepan, place over high heat, and bring to a boil. Remove from the heat and pour through a fine-mesh sieve into a heatproof bowl or other heatproof container. Set aside.

Return the Dutch oven to medium heat. Add the vegetables to the hot oil and brown well on all sides, about 10 minutes. Dust the vegetables with the cocoa powder and mix well.

continued

Place the chicken pieces on top of the vegetables and pour the strained marinade over them. Bring to a boil over medium-high heat, cover, and place in the oven. Cook until the chicken is tender and its juices run clear when the meat is pricked with a knife tip, 30 to 45 minutes.

Remove the chicken to a large warmed platter or shallow bowl and cover to keep warm. Pour the contents of the Dutch oven through a fine-mesh sieve placed over a saucepan and, reserving the vegetables, season the liquid to taste with salt and pepper. Add the mushrooms and place over medium-high heat. Bring to a boil and boil for 5 minutes; the sauce will reduce and thicken slightly and the mushrooms will be tender.

Meanwhile, bring a large pot of salted water to a boil, add the macaroni, and cook until al dente, according to package instructions. Drain well.

To serve, divide the macaroni, the chicken pieces, and the vegetables evenly among warmed individual plates and pour the mushrooms and sauce over the top. Garnish the sauce with a little parsley and serve at once.

Serves 8

COWGIRL CREAMERY'S MT. TAM, PARMIGIANO-REGGIANO, AND SONOMA DRY JACK

An elegant cheese course follows naturally on the heels of the rustic Coq au Vin. Arranged artfully on a platter, Cowgirl Creamery's Mt. Tam, a sophisticated triple cream; toothsome Parmigiano-Reggiano; and bold, nutty Sonoma Dry Jack make a satisfying trio. A fine older red such as the 1995 Jordan Cabernet Sauvignon, with its rich and varied flavors, complements the cheeses and provides a complex tasting experience.

A selection of fine cheeses.

> *Decanting is the final brush stroke on the canvas of a fine wine.*
>
> *The art of decanting allows the artistic nuances to appear.*
>
> —JESS JACKSON and BARBARA BANKE, Proprietors, Kendall Jackson Vineyard Estate, Sonoma, California

HOT CHOCOLATE CAKES WITH STRAWBERRY SALAD

These simple-to-make individual chocolate cakes, served with ripe red strawberries tossed with Grand Marnier, will please nearly any palate and bring a fine meal to a memorable finish. Use the highest-quality dark chocolate you can find, preferably one that is at least 66 percent cacao, such as Valrhona's bittersweet Caraïbe.

Preheat the oven to 325 degrees F. Butter eight ½-cup ramekins, then dust with flour and tap out the excess. Arrange the ramekins on a baking sheet.

In the top pan of a double boiler, combine the butter and chocolate. Place over barely simmering water and heat just until melted. Remove from the heat and stir until smooth.

Whisk the sugar, eggs, and salt into the chocolate mixture until well blended. Using the tip of a knife, scrape the seeds from the vanilla bean into the mixture and discard the pod. Whisk again until well mixed. Quickly stir in the flour just until blended.

Divide the batter evenly among the prepared ramekins, filling them three-fourths full. Bake until edges are set but the centers are still very wet, about 10 minutes.

While the cakes are baking, make the strawberry salad: In a bowl, combine the strawberries, sugar, and Grand Marnier and toss gently to mix.

Remove the cakes from the oven and let cool in the ramekins for 5 minutes. To unmold each cake, carefully run a thin-bladed knife around the inside edge of the ramekin, and then invert the cake onto an individual plate and sprinkle with gold leaf. (The center will be very soft and will "bleed" when cut.) Place a spoonful of the strawberry salad alongside and serve immediately.

Serves 8

FOR THE CAKES:

½ cup plus 3 tablespoons unsalted butter, plus butter for pan

6 ounces bittersweet chocolate, broken into pieces

½ cup sugar

4 large eggs

Pinch of salt

½ vanilla bean, split lengthwise

4 tablespoons plus 2 teaspoons all-purpose flour, sifted

Feuille d'or (edible gold leaf) for serving

FOR THE STRAWBERRY SALAD:

2½ cups strawberries, hulled and sliced

2 tablespoons sugar

2½ tablespoons Grand Marnier

From decanting to toasting and tasting, the traditions of wine presentation are honored by expert sommeliers and wine lovers everywhere. Including them in one's own dining rituals will do more than improve the taste of a wine and impress guests. It will connect today's host with those who have practiced the art of decanting throughout the centuries, bringing together good friends, good food, and exceptional wine.

EPILOGUE

As a winemaker, I have the pleasure of seeing a wine's progress from the very beginning—from the day the vines are pruned, to the cool early morning when the grapes are harvested, to the afternoon when we transfer the young wine to oak casks, to the day it is poured into the bottle for aging. The hands of many artisans are represented here. Some might think that the winemaking process ends at the moment of uncorking. But, in fact, the wine's journey does not end until it is lovingly, carefully decanted into a finely crafted decanter, when it finally makes itself ready to be tasted and enjoyed. The privilege, the responsibility, of performing this final step falls to you, the wine lover. In so doing, you give the wine this careful preparation it so richly deserves, before it is poured into those waiting glasses.

The ancient Greeks observed that the soul of man is the exercise of the senses: sight, touch, smell, taste, and hearing. Decanting allows us to fully enjoy the sensual experience of tasting a wine as it completes its journey from young grape to mature, complex elixir. In this way, we make a soulful connection with ourselves, with the winemakers, and with our loved ones with whom we share this unique beverage. Decanting, like good wine, and like good living, is indeed an art, one to be shared with all who aspire to live life at its grandest.

Rob Davis

Rob Davis
Winemaker, Jordan Vineyard & Winery

ACKNOWLEDGMENTS

Researching, writing, and photographing *The Art of Decanting* has been
a wonderful and stimulating project.

I would like to acknowledge my fellow coworkers at Jordan: Rob Davis,
Lisbeth Holmefjord, Udo Nechutnys, Todd Knoll, Betty Burg, and John Kozubal.
Jill Young and her staff at Young|Wells were also invaluable in this project,
as was the photography of Caitlin McCaffrey, whose consideration and
thoughtfulness was essential in making this endeavor a success. Nina Wemyss'
historical expertise was of great importance, as was Lindsey Lee Johnson's
contribution. They were all wonderfully enthusiastic and helpful.

One of the extra joys of this work was to be in contact, once again, with good
friends who graciously agreed to share their well recognized-wine expertise.
I take this opportunity to express our thanks for their help.

BIBLIOGRAPHY

Asher, Gerald. *Vineyard Tales: Reflections on Wine.* San Francisco: Chronicle Books, 1996.

Beech, Charlotte, and Abigail Hole. *Lonely Planet Portugal.* Victoria, Australia: Lonely Planet, 2005.

Bober, Phyllis Pray. Art, *Culture, sine: Ancient and Medieval Gastronomy.* Chicago: University of Chicago Press, 1999.

Butler, Robin, and Gillian Walkling. *The Book of Wine Antiques.* Suffolk, UK: Antique Collectors' Club, 1995.

Byron, Lord. *Sardanapalus, a Tragedy.* In *Sardanapalus, a Tragedy; The Two Foscari, a Tragedy; Cain, a Mystery.* London: John Murray, 1821.

Chardin, John. *Travels in Persia: 1673–1677.* Mineola, NY: Dover Publications, 1988.

Chernow, Ron. *Alexander Hamilton.* New York: Penguin Press, 2004.

Commander's Palace, New Orleans, Louisiana, wine list (courtesy of John McDonald, Dallas, Texas).

Cook, Robert M. *Greek Painted Pottery.* London: Routledge, 1997.

Dame, Fred. "Screwing Around: Screw Caps vs. Cork—Which Way Would You Go?" *Novus Vinum.* www.novusvinum.com.

Day, Charles William. *Hints on Etiquette and the Usages of Society: With a Glance at Bad Habits.* Boston: W. D. Ticknor, 1844.

Dickens, Charles. *A Christmas Carol.* Mineola, NY: Courier Dover Publications, 1991.

Dougherty, Carol. "The Aristonothos Krater: Competing Stories of Conflict and Collaboration." Chap. 3 in *The Cultures Within Ancient Greek Culture: Contact, Conflict, Collaboration.* Edited by Carol Doughtery and Leslie Kurke. Cambridge: Cambridge University Press, 2003.

Dumas, Alexandre. *The Romances of Alexandre Dumas.* Little Brown and Co., 1898.

Ellis, Roger. *Who's Who in British History: Victorian Britain, 1851–1901.* Mechanicsburg, PA: Stackpole Books, 1997.

Emert, Carol. "Riedel—The Wine Glass with a Brain." *San Francisco Chronicle,* August 28, 2003, sec. D2.

Flanders, Judith. *Inside the Victorian Home: A Portrait of Domestic Life in Victorian England.* New York: W. W. Norton and Company, 2003.

Foulkes, Christopher, ed. *Larousse Encyclopedia of Wine.* London: Hamlyn, 2001.

Franklin, Benjamin. *The Works of Benjamin Franklin.* Chicago: T. MacCoun, 1882.

Gaiter, Dorothy J., and John Brecher. "Decanters Are Nice Gifts, but Do You Need Them?" *The Wall Street Journal Online,* April 25, 2003.

Gentleman. *The Laws of Etiquette: or, Short Rules and Reflections for Conduct in Society.* Philadelphia: Carey, Lea, and Blanchard, 1836.

Gilbey. *The Compleat Imbiber.* London: W. and A. Gilbey, 1957.

Hancock, David. "'A Revolution in the Trade': Wine Distribution and the Development of the Infrastructure of the Atlantic Market Economy, 1703–1807." Chap. 5 in *The Early Modern Atlantic Economy.* Edited by John J. McCusker and Kenneth Morgan. Cambridge: Cambridge University Press, 2000.

Harrison, Babs. *The Art of Wine.* Philadelphia: Running Press, 2001.

Inch, Arthur, and Arlene Hirst. *Dinner Is Served: An English Butler's Guide to the Art of the Table.* Philadelphia: Running Press, 2003.

Jefferson, Thomas. *Memoir, Correspondence, and Miscellanies.* Charlottesville, VA: F. Carr and Co., 1829.

Johnson, Hugh. *How to Enjoy Wine.* New York: Fireside, 1985.

———. *The Story of Wine.* New Illustrated Edition. London: Mitchell Beazley, 2004.

Johnson, Hugh, Dora Jane Janson, and David Revere McFadden. *Wine: Celebration and Ceremony.* New York: Cooper-Hewitt Museum, 1985.

Joseph, Robert, and Margaret Rand. *The Keep It Simple Series Guide to Wine.* New York: DK Publishing, 2000.

Kincaid, Les. "Decanting Wines." *Les Kincaid Wine,* 2001–2003. www.leskincaid.com.

———. "To Cellar and to Serve." *Les Kincaid Wine,* 2001–2004. www.leskincaid.com.

McGovern, Patrick E. *Ancient Wine: The Search for the Origins of Viticulture.* Princeton, NJ: Princeton University Press, 2003.

Mondavi, Robert. *Harvests of Joy: How the Good Life Became Great Business.* New York: Harcourt Brace, 1998.

Monticello Explorer. "Seau Crénelé." *Monticello Explorer,* www.monticello.org.

Morton, Agnes H. *Etiquette: Good Manners for All People, Especially for Those 'Who Dwell Within the Broad Zone of the Average'.* Philadelphia: Penn Publishing Company, 1909.

Newman, Paul B. *Daily Life in the Middle Ages.* Jefferson, NC: McFarland and Company, 2001.

New Zealand Screwcap Wine Seal Initiative. "Technical Information." www.screwcap.co.nz.

Peynaud, Emile. *The Taste of Wine: The Art and Science of Wine Appreciation.* San Francisco: Wine Appreciation Guild, 1996.

Riedel, Georg. "Shape and Pleasure: 'The Content Determines the Shape.'" www.riedel.com.

Simon, L. André. *Bottlescrew Days.* London: Duckworth, 1926.

Sogg, Daniel. "Decanting: Aeration—Friend and Enemy of Wine." *Wine Spectator,* November 15, 2003.

Sydney, William Connor. *England and the English in the Eighteenth Century: Chapters in the Social History of the Times.* London: Ward and Downey, 1891.

Symons, Michael. *A History of Cooks and Cooking.* Champaign, IL: University of Illinois Press, 2004.

U.S. War Department. *Annual Reports of the War Department for the Fiscal Year Ended June 30, 1902, Volume I, Report of the Secretary of War and Reports of Bureau Chiefs.* Washington, DC: Government Printing Office, 1903.

Wilcox, Beagan. "A Corking Dilemma." *Forbes,* July 31, 2002.

X, Countess of. "The Private Apartments at Windsor Castle." *The English Illustrated Magazine,* April to September 1904.

PHOTO AND ILLUSTRATION CREDITS

© **Baccarat**: p. 82–83.

© **The Bridgeman Art Library**: p. 17 © British Museum, London, UK/The Bridgeman Art Library, *Banquet Scene*, part of a wall painting from the tomb-chapel of Nebamun, Thebes, New Kingdom, c. 1350 b.c. (painted plaster) by Egyptian, 18th Dynasty (c. 1567–1320 b.c.); p. 18 © Musée de la Ville de Paris, Musée du Petit-Palais, France/Lauros/Giraudon/The Bridgeman Art Library, Fol.298r *How the Noble King Alexander Was Poisoned*, illustration from a book by Jean Wauquelin, 1460 (vellum) by French School (15th century); p. 19 © Ashmolean Museum, University of Oxford, UK/The Bridgeman Art Library, Attic red-figure cup decorated with a naked slave-girl holding a wine cup and a ladle, by Otlos, c. 510 b.c. (ceramic); p. 19 © Ashmolean Museum, University of Oxford, UK/The Bridgeman Art Library, Attic red-figure stamnos decorated with women serving wine and making music, by the Villa Painter, Greek (ceramic); p. 45 © Yale Center for British Art, Paul Mellon Collection, USA, *The Brothers Clarke with Other Gentlemen Taking Wine*, c. 1730–35, oil on canvas, Gawen Hamilton (c. 1697–1737); p. 55 © Private Collection, Bonhams, London, UK/ The Bridgeman Art Library, *A Satisfying Meal*, 1883 (oil on canvas) by Charles Meer Webb (1830–95); p. 67 © Private Collection/The Bridgeman Art Library, *Manufacture of Bottle Corks*, from the 'Encyclopedie des Sciences et Metiers' by Denis Diderot (1713–84), published c. 1770 (engraving), French School (18th century); p. 87 © Musée des Beaux-Arts, Rouen, France/Lauros/Giraudon/The Bridgeman Art Library, *The Wedding Meal at Yport*, 1886 (oil on canvas) by Albert-Auguste Fourie (b. 1854); p. 104 © National Museum and Gallery of Wales, Cardiff/The Bridgeman Art Library, *The Bachelor's Breakfast Table*, 1885 (oil on panel) by Joseph Benwell Clark (1857–c. 1880).

© **Avelina Crespo**: p. 68 (glass bottle stoppers/ Sandra Jordan Collection).

© **Caitlin McCaffrey**: Cover; Inside Front Cover; p. 6; p. 8; p. 14; p. 16 Private Collection of Margrit and Robert Mondavi; p. 21 (top and bottom) decanter courtesy of Riedel; p. 22 Collection of Rob Davis; p. 27; p. 31; p. 32; p. 34; p. 36; p. 38 Private Collection of Margrit and Robert Mondavi; p. 39 Private Collection of Margrit and Robert Mondavi; p. 40 Private Collection of Margrit and Robert Mondavi; p. 41 Private Collection of Margrit and Robert Mondavi; p. 42 Private Collection of Margrit and Robert Mondavi; p. 44; p. 46; p. 47 Private Collection of Margrit and Robert Mondavi; p. 49; p. 50; p. 51; p. 52; p. 56; p. 57; p. 58; p. 59; p. 62; p. 64; p. 65; p. 66; p. 70; p. 71; p. 72; p. 75; p. 76 wineglasses courtesy of Gump's; p. 78 wineglass courtesy of Baccarat; p. 79 Private Collection of Margrit and Robert Mondavi; p. 81 wineglass courtesy of Gump's; p. 84 wineglass courtesy of Gump's; p. 85 wineglass courtesy of Gump's; p. 86 wineglass courtesy of Gump's; p. 88; p. 90; p. 91; p. 92; p. 93; p. 94; p. 95; p. 97; p. 98; p. 101; p. 105; p. 106; p. 109; p. 110 Manuel Reyes, Sous Chef, Jordan Vineyard & Winery; p. 113; p. 114; p. 117; p. 118; p. 121; p. 122.

INDEX

A

Amphorae, 16, 38, 41, 64, 67
Aumbries, 19, 100

B

Bottles, 42–44, 47

C

Cakes, Hot Chocolate, with Strawberry Salad, 120
Cellaring, 48, 51
Cheese course, 119
Chicken
    Coq au Vin, 116, 119
Chocolate Cakes, Hot, with Strawberry Salad, 120
Coasters, 30, 32–33
Coolers, 54–58, 61
Coq au Vin, 116, 119
Corks, 64–69, 72, 74–75
Corkscrews, 64, 69–71, 75

D

Decanters, 21, 43–44, 47
Decanting
    accessories for, 30, 32–35
    effects of, 11–12, 23, 25–26, 29
    history of, 16, 19–21
    technique of, 26, 30–31

F

Funnels, 30, 33–35
Furnishings, 100–105

G

Glass
bottles and decanters, 42–47, 67–68
stoppers, 68

K

Kraters, 16, 19, 41

M

Madeira, 20–21
Monteiths, 58–60
Mushrooms
    Coq au Vin, 116, 119
    Roasted Sweet Onions with Chanterelle Mushrooms, 112, 115

O

Onions, Roasted Sweet, with Chanterelle Mushrooms, 112, 115
Oysters, BeauSoleil, with Ponzu Sauce, 112

P

Port, 20

R

Rafraichissoirs, 102, 103, 104
Recipes, 112–20

S

Screw caps, 74–75
Seau crénelé, 58, 60
Shallot-Herb Butter, 115
Sideboards, 100, 103–5
Side tables, 100
Strawberry Salad, Hot Chocolate Cakes with, 120

T

Tannin, 93
Tasses jumelles, 93, 95
Tastevins, 93, 95
Tasting, 90–96
TCA, 72, 74
Toasting, 86

W

Wine. *See also* Decanting
    blending, 16, 19
    cellaring, 48, 51
    chilling, 54–58, 60–61
    pairing food with, 108
    serving, 60–61, 81, 84–85
    tasting, 90–96
    uncorking, 64, 70, 72
    vessels for, 38–47
Wine coolers, 54–58, 61
Wineglasses
    chilling, 58, 60
    ideal, 78, 80
    placement of, 84
    types of, 78–86
Wine tables, 102, 104